The voluntary sector delivering public services

Available in alternative formats

This publication can be provided in alternative formats, such as large print, Braille, audiotape and on disk. Please contact:
Communications Department, Joseph Rowntree Foundation, The Homestead, 40 Water End, York YO30 6WP.
Tel: 01904 615905. Email: info@jrf.org.uk

The voluntary sector delivering public services

Transfer or transformation?

Will Paxton and Nick Pearce
Julia Unwin and Peter Molyneux

JOSEPH ROWNTREE
FOUNDATION

The **Joseph Rowntree Foundation** has supported this project as part of its programme of research and innovative development projects, which it hopes will be of value to policy makers, practitioners and service users. The facts presented and views expressed in this report are, however, those of the authors and not necessarily those of the Foundation.

Joseph Rowntree Foundation
The Homestead
40 Water End
York YO30 6WP
Website: www.jrf.org.uk

© Part I IPPR 2005
© Part II Julia Unwin Consultancy 2005
© This collection Joseph Rowntree Foundation 2005

First published 2005 by the Joseph Rowntree Foundation

ISBN 1 85935 367 3   (paperback)
ISBN 1 85935 368 1   (pdf: available at www.jrf.org.uk)

A CIP catalogue record for this report is available from the British Library.

Cover design by Adkins Design

Prepared and printed by:
York Publishing Services Ltd
64 Hallfield Road
Layerthorpe
York
YO31 7ZQ
Tel: 01904 430033   Fax: 01904 430868   Website: www.yps-publishing.co.uk

Further copies of this report, or any other JRF publication, can be obtained either from the JRF website (www.jrf.org.uk/bookshop/) or from our distributor, York Publishing Services Ltd, at the above address.

CONTENTS

PART II BEYOND TRANSFER TO TRANSFORMATION
Julia Unwin and Peter Molyneux

FOREWORD BY RICHARD BEST

As Will Paxton and Nick Pearce point out in Part I of this report, there are two big reasons for government to engineer the transfer of more public services to the voluntary and community sector (VCS): first, to modernise public services by bringing in the pluralism, competition, variety, innovation and flexibility associated with this sector; second, and linked, to engage more citizens and more communities directly in the process of service delivery, reform of state-funded services and more widespread civil renewal.

To strengthen the VCS, the government is bringing in better regulatory arrangements through the Charities Bill, infrastructure support through the Home Office HUB programmes and funding through 'Futurebuilders', alongside encouragement to local authorities and others to transfer services to the VCS. But will these changes fulfil the government's hopes? Will they lead to a real transformation in service provision? And what will they do for the future of the voluntary sector?

The authors of Part I recognise the value of the VCS delivering public services, but suggest that government is less concerned about the VCS being equipped to take forward the civil renewal agenda. They make important recommendations on how this second half of the equation can be given more emphasis.

In Part II of the report, Julia Unwin and Peter Molyneux suggest the voluntary sector should do more than simply run public services more effectively. They show the ways in which very different organisations – responsible for museums, transport and waste management, housing, health and social care – can really transform a particular service, not least by making the key link to the users of the services. They show it is possible for the VCS both to deliver a modernised, diversified public service and to give users and communities a much better role in the process. But it takes a lot of commitment on all sides.

The biggest example of a shift of public service provision to the voluntary sector is in the housing field: first, funding for new social housing was switched from councils to housing associations in the 1980s; then large-scale transfers of council stock followed wherever tenants voted for this. JRF's research suggests that few tenants or staff would wish to reverse these trends.

But the story has now moved on: in place of a plurality of organisations offering choice and flexibility, government is concentrating its funding, through the Housing Corporation, on a smaller and smaller number of very large Registered Social Landlords. The latest plan is to achieve further 'efficiency gains' by switching social housing grants for new housing to unregulated, profit-making, housebuilders and developers. This suggests that the agenda may ultimately be propelled by the Treasury with an eye on short-term savings. And talk of the inherent advantages of a strong, non profit, socially motivated voluntary and community sector – which locks in government grants for public benefit in perpetuity – is no protection against onward transfer of services to the private sector if that pays quicker dividends.

The VCS will need to assert more vehemently its intrinsic value to society, to consumers and to users, if it is not to be simply a stepping stone from the public to the private sector. This report helps to make the case and the JRF is very grateful to its four authors and to our own Maggie Jones for pulling it together.

Part I

The voluntary sector and the state

Will Paxton and Nick Pearce

1 INTRODUCTION

The voluntary and community sector (VCS) is at a crossroads. In recent years it has expanded the role it plays in the direct delivery of public services and this shift has received sustained and continuing support across the political spectrum. But are we clear about why such an expanded role is desirable? Should we want the VCS to continue to expand its role in public service provision? What are the risks if this were to happen?

This paper explores these questions with reference to two strands of thinking. The first strand, which focuses on reform of the state, stresses the need to fashion a more plural, democratic and responsive state to replace one which is overly centralised and bureaucratic. This approach primarily sees the VCS as a potential provider of public services. The second strand of thought is one that policy makers and politicians have rediscovered in recent years: one which emphasises the value of 'community' and 'civil renewal'. The VCS is central to most discussions of this too.

On the face of it these two debates could generate contradictory implications for the relationship between the state and VCS: one driving them towards greater integration, the other emphasising separation and the distinct value of the VCS as part of civil society. It is this apparent tension which this paper seeks to address. There may be times when policy makers can square this circle and combine an increased role for the VCS in public service delivery with the promotion of a stronger civil society, but at others there may be direct trade-offs and tough decisions to be made.

The argument of the paper

The paper is divided into three sections. In the first we discuss how to define the VCS and outline the state reform argument for the VCS taking a greater role in service delivery. We also briefly discuss the policy changes which have flowed from this thinking and identify some key trends in the VCS. The emerging approach to public administration of 'public value' is stressed; this is an approach which could support a further expansion of the VCS's role in service delivery in the future.

But this should not be the sole focus for policy makers. In the second section we argue that a relationship between the VCS and the state, derived from a concern for 'community' or 'civil renewal', may result in different policy implications, or at a minimum a difference of emphasis as policy develops in this area. It would suggest that there is a danger that too much emphasis is placed on the role of the VCS *vis-à-vis* debates about reform of the state and that not enough consideration is given to how the state could act to foster a strong VCS as part of a strong civil society.

In the final section we conclude that while the VCS does have a crucial role to play in the direct provision of public services, a more balanced and nuanced approach would be generated by thinking about the sector (and government's relationships with it), through a civil renewal lens as well as in terms of state reform. We highlight the need to develop better local 'civic infrastructures' as a way of ensuring the state provides the right form of support for the VCS. There should be a reconsideration of the existing, somewhat arbitrary, government target in this area and a refocusing of government action, funding and energy. Further research should focus on how the VCS can deliver more public services, but do so without compromising the very qualities which could help it play an important role in the wider civil renewal agenda.

2 WHERE ARE WE STARTING FROM?

Defining the voluntary and community sector

Defining the VCS is notoriously difficult. We deliberately do not seek to be overly precise in this paper. Indeed, the government itself has often failed to nail down a specific definition and instead has stressed the sector's heterogeneity. In 2002 the Treasury argued that the VCS was 'wider in scope than "general charities" and the "voluntary sector", inclusive of organisations reflecting the characteristics of social enterprise, but narrower in scope than "non-profit", "third sector" or "social economy"' (HM Treasury, 2002, p. 7). The picture is further complicated, and any definition broadened, by the development of new forms of voluntary association – foundation hospitals being one such recent development. We will follow the government's inclusive definition and assume that organisations and associations which are neither part of the state nor in the private sector should be seen as being part of the VCS. Such a definition would link the VCS closely with at least one common understanding of 'civil society' (see Edwards, 2004 for further discussion).

Under any definition it is important to emphasise, as the government does, that the VCS is heterogeneous. Voluntary and community organisations (VCOs) can be more or less *formally* organised – some are well established and permanent while others may be formed on an ad hoc basis and be only temporary.

They can be more or less *independent* (see Kendall and Knapp, 1993 for further discussion). They can be more or less grounded in *voluntarism*. They can, for example, either have a large number of volunteers or be largely professionalised. They may have different key *objectives*: some may provide a service, some may exist to provide a 'public benefit' while others will act as pressure group. Lastly VCOs come in a variety of *different sizes* ranging from small organisations based in just one community to larger organisations with national (or even global) reach.

Just as it is difficult to define the VCS as an entire sector, it is hard to use these different variables to make clear distinctions between different segments of the VCS. It is not easy, for example, simply to make a divide between (smaller) 'community-based' organisations and (larger) 'voluntary' organisations. But there are differences and it is clear that some organisations are more suited than others to providing public services and entering into contractual relationships with the state. These are likely to be larger, and more professional and have a service provision role. Many other parts of the VCS will be less suited to providing public services. These organisations are more likely to rely on volunteers, be less professional, have less expertise with delivery of public services and be more independent. Though making this distinction is not straightforward, the crucial point is that for large parts of the VCS debates about delivering public services are not generally relevant (Dekker and van den Broek, 1998). Nevertheless this has been the focus of recent policy.

A dominant strand of thinking: reform of the modern state

The main intellectual driver behind the expansion of the role of the VCS in public service delivery is a desire, on both sides of

British politics, to reform the traditional command-and-control state. In the post-war period, a centralised and top-down state was regarded by many as the most appropriate way of securing social and economic change. Aneurin Bevan, the founding father of the National Health Service, who famously wanted the sound of a bedpan dropped on any NHS ward to reverberate around Whitehall, would very probably have been horrified by some recent suggestions that have been made about the potential role of the VCS in helping to fashion a more plural, democratic and responsive state. For Bevan's supporters the vagaries and inconsistencies of pre-war welfare provision could only be eliminated by a strong central state (although he chose local government to deliver the huge post-war increase in social housing). But for contemporary government thinkers, a challenging examination of this tradition is now seen as necessary even if that means the VCS delivering 'core' parts of the public services. (See, for example, the speech given by Alan Milburn to the 2004 ACEVO [Association of Chief Executives of Voluntary Organisations] conference). *In extremis*, they argue that the future legitimacy of state action is at stake and that the public services are in a race for survival.

It was the political right that first developed a popular and effective critique of the post-war centralised state, arguing that it was unresponsive, inefficient and undermined personal liberty. Although Thatcher had less impact on the size and nature of government than is often assumed, the 1980s did alter fundamentally the terms of debate. Big questions about the role of the state in society, indeed questions about the very nature of the state, were firmly on the agenda. The use of quasi markets, particularly in education and health, with divides *within* the state sector between purchasers and providers; the introduction of Next Steps agencies, at arm's length from the state, to help improve performance; and attempts to ensure a plurality of providers in

8

areas previously seen as the reserve of public providers are all now familiar issues in debates about public policy.

It is largely in this context, where a battle for the future shape and nature of the state is being fought, that debates about the VCS delivering public services should be seen. The last point raised above, regarding a plurality of providers, is most relevant. Though the political right was first to develop a coherent critique of the centralised post-war welfare state, since 1997 the Labour government has continually emphasised the importance of 'what works'. Desperate to defend the principle of universal public services and to meet the growing demands of an increasingly affluent and discriminating electorate, experimentation with Public Private Partnerships (PPPs), measured in terms of media and policy interest at least, has been central to debates about the future of public services (Kelly, 2000). If a plurality of providers, including the VCS, is thought to drive up standards and increase choice, then it has been encouraged.

Indeed the VCS is considered to provide a specific added value. This value may be derived from the facts that VCOs are more likely to be driven by a specific sense of mission; that they may have niche skills and expertise; that they have greater 'proximity' to users; and are more able to innovate and provide services flexibly (see Bolton, 2003 for a fuller discussion on 'value added' and Billis and Glennerster, 1998 for a useful welfare economists' perspective). Indeed there is reason to believe that policy makers will become more aware of the potential added value of the VCS. Witness developments in theories of public administration: New Public Management, the vogue in the 1980s and still the orthodox approach to public management, sees accountability as upwards through contracts or outwards towards *consumers*. As such it stresses performance targets set by the centre and relies on consumerist forms of consultation.

In contrast a new approach, which finds some favour in central government, is that of 'public value'. This provides a broader measure than is conventionally used with more emphasis on outcomes and the means used to deliver outcomes, as well as trust and legitimacy. As a result the emphasis is on wider collective objectives arrived at through deliberation; accountability out to the public in various ways – as citizens, as customers or as taxpayers; and reduced reliance on performance targets at the expense of greater public consultation (Kelly *et al.*, 2002). Because the VCS can often claim to be better at consulting and engaging citizens and because it is likely to be more trusted, a public value framework may make it more attractive as a service provider.

There is then a strong case for policy enabling the VCS to deliver more public services. Public value may strengthen this case. Below we outline some of the implications of this dominant strand of thinking, but also highlight the risks it poses. In Chapter 3 we outline another philosophical tradition which can lead to different implications for the relationship between the VCS and the state.

Recent policy and trends in the sector

Largely because of a desire to use the VCS to improve service delivery, particularly in some specific areas of the public sector, the last decade has witnessed significant policy activity. Since 1997 there have been government reviews (two Treasury-led 'cross-cutting reviews'[1]); targets (the Home Office has a Public Service Agreement [PSA] target to increase the VCS contribution to public service delivery[2]); dedicated funding streams (the Futurebuilders fund, intended primarily to help achieve this target) and a dedicated unit in government (the Active Communities Unit). The vast majority of this attention has been focused on the role of the VCS in directly delivering public services.

There has also been a significant increase in state funding of the VCS. Between 1991 and 2001, VCS income from government increased by nearly 40 per cent. In 1999/2000 the amount of state funding received by the VCS, including both direct funding and funding via agencies or non-departmental public bodies, was £1.1 billion. At the same time the overall VCS has continued to grow, though at a slower pace than a decade ago. It is difficult to break down these figures in detail by different parts of the sector, but we can see how different-sized organisations are affected. Caution is required, but size can be used as a proxy for other differences – levels of professionalism, core objectives and so on. Larger organisations receive higher levels of earned income and they receive more of this from government. Smaller organisations, by comparison, receive a greater amount of voluntary income.[3] In 2001/02 the largest charities, defined as those with a turnover of over £10 million, received 22.8 per cent of their income from contracts with government. In contrast those with turnovers of between £10,000 and £100,000 received only 4.8 per cent of their income from government. For the smallest organisations, with turnovers of under £10,000, the figure was even lower at 0.8 per cent (NCVO, 2004). Overall the trend is upwards – there was a 9 per cent increase between 2000/01 and 2001/02. This raises risks for the VCS, many of which have been well documented. Three of these are:

1   *Trust:* In an era of growing mistrust in many public
    institutions, there is still at least the perception of higher
    levels of trust in the VCS. Indeed trust is crucial if the sector
    is seen as a vehicle for people's participation in civil society.
    Trust, however, is hard to regain once lost, and any erosion
    will have long-lasting repercussions (Anheier and Romo,
    1992). Although there is little hard empirical evidence, the
    clear danger is that closer relationships with the state will

undermine levels of trust. As VCOs become more professional a tension may grow between 'doing good' in an ethical sense and 'doing well' in an organisational sense that may harden trust relationships (see Tonkiss and Passey, 1999 for further discussion).

2 *Independence:* If the VCS relies more on state funding and the delivery of public services, it runs the risk of compromising its independence. Political influence and regulation, often exercised indirectly through funding, may alter the core objectives focus of VCOs to reflect wider government objectives (Petrella, 2001). Demands for professionalism may affect governance arrangements – how an organisation operates at a practical level – as well as its core objectives. All of this can compromise perceived independence (see DiMaggio and Powell, 1983 for further discussion).

3 *Dilution of mission:* VCOs are distinguished by their 'values expressive' character. It is possible that management in a values expressive organisation is distinguished by how the organisation goes about setting and attaining specific goals. Closer VCS relations with the state could bring discontinuity between 'espoused purpose and values' and 'operative purposes and values' (Jeavons, 1992, p. 410).

The blurring of boundaries between different sectors – public and private, public and voluntary – does raise salient questions about the reform of the state. One controversial issue is whether or not there are some 'core' public services which should not be provided by the VCS. For example, should the state want the VCS to run schools? The recent introduction of Community

Interest Companies (CICs) as a possible vehicle for VCS delivery of public services make these debates highly salient. The Treasury and the Chancellor have been keen to draw boundaries around core public services, but how robustly such lines can be drawn remains far from clear.

This is a crucial issue for government, but it is the implications for the VCS which this paper focuses on. How will a closer relationship with the state, whether delivering 'core' public services or not, affect the VCS itself? Is there a trade-off between trying to achieve a more plural state and ensuring that organisations which become more closely 'integrated' with the state do not lose their distinctive characteristics? For the private sector this is less of an issue. It is not being asked to fundamentally change its *modus operandi*, but simply to contract with the state rather than within the private market. But for the VCS more difficult questions arise. Will the distinctive role of the VCS in civil society be undermined? It is a key concern that when the VCS is involved in delivering public services the very sources of added value, or of 'public value', that made them a suitable provider will be eroded. How can we maximise the chances of the VCS retaining its sources of added value when it delivers public services?

3   AN ALTERNATIVE APPROACH

Without dismissing the potential role of the VCS in service delivery or an expanded role in the future, policy makers need to place these debates in a wider context. There is a danger of focusing too much on service delivery without recognising the impact this could have on the VCS or addressing the wider goals represented by another tradition of thought – one which looks through a civil society or 'civil renewal' lens. In this section we outline in more detail this other philosophical lens through which VCS/state relationships could be framed. We suggest that this should be given more weight.

Civil renewal and the voluntary and community sector

At the same time as thinkers have pondered the nature of the modern state, they have developed a stronger account of the value of civil society and associational life. Civil society has always existed and many strands of progressive thinking have emphasised the importance of local, bottom-up forms of active citizenship. From de Tocqueville's 'little platoons' through to Thomas Paine's American Revolution-inspired republicanism, and from the functional socialism of Harold Laski to the Guild Socialism of G.D.H. Cole, the vitality of civil society has, in differing ways, been a clear element of much progressive thought. Recently some of these strands of thought have been rediscovered. Many modern politicians now talk of the importance of 'community' and 'active citizenship'. In recent decades there have been falls in key measures of citizen participation, for example voting and membership of political parties, which have led some to call for policy which seeks to 'renew' civil society. The VCS, as the site of much associational life, is at the heart of these debates.

The importance of associational life and the vitality of civil society have experienced a renaissance in academia and policy circles in recent years. There are many competing arguments about both the definition of civil society and why strengthening it (or at least not harming it) might be considered a desirable goal of public policy. In this paper we adopt an approach and definition which draw heavily on the civic republican strand of thinking. This approach appears to match the views held by senior government ministers. For example the former Home Secretary, David Blunkett, published a pamphlet in 2003 in which he noted approvingly that: 'In recent years there has been a surge of interest amongst political theorists in civic republican thinking, often associated with communitarian philosophers such as Michael Sandel, Quentin Skinner and Charles Taylor, but also overlapping with strong currents of social capital theory' (Blunkett, 2003, p. 5). Likewise the present Chancellor argued in a recent speech that 'civic society' was a core element of Britishness (Brown, 2004). The government believes that democratic and wider civic participation is an important element of what it is to be a full citizen, and that inspiration is drawn from civic republican writing.

Such thought is grounded in a belief that citizens should play an active role in the political life (generally widely defined as far more than simply voting or being a member of a political association) of their community and nation. Theorists vary according to why this is considered important. At one end of the spectrum civic republican thinkers would argue that it is only in

ion that citizens can achieve the highest form of life.
famously argued that only beasts and gods could live
without politics. Civic republican thinkers have also drawn on the
writings of Jean-Jacques Rousseau, who saw citizens' interests
as intrinsically tied up with that of the 'common will' or the state.
At the other end of the spectrum is a somewhat more liberal
view, articulated amongst others by Machiavelli and Dagger, which
contends that citizens must actively participate in the governance
of their community because this is the only way to ensure that
the state does not become too overbearing (Pettit, 1997).

The contemporary politicians mentioned above would be closer
to the more liberal end of this spectrum, though probably slightly
less suspicious of state action. But wherever on the spectrum
people fall similar policy implications are derived: first, citizens
should participate in the governance of their communities and
nation and there must be a variety of routes to such participation,
not just formal representative democracy; second, community is
an important value which must be protected; and third, people
must be trained, in a variety of ways, to be active citizens. This
last point is important. Put another way, it demands that citizens
cultivate civic virtues, which may cover both a sense of civility or
regard for the interests of others and also, in a stronger sense, a
sense of civic responsibility – of citizens working together for the
common good (Dagger, 1997).

In all the three areas mentioned above the VCS remains crucial.

1 *Route to participation:* The VCS can provide a route for
   people to get involved in both voluntary action and wider
   governance of local communities. It can, for example, allow
   service users to channel their opinions and demands to
   service providers. This process is being formalised with the
   emphasis on 'partnership' and a shift from local *government*

to local *governance*. Witness, for example, the introduction of Local Strategic Partnerships, on which the VCS is represented. This is particularly the case for those living in deprived areas and for whom traditional forms of democratic participation are either closed or less appealing.

2   *Communities and social capital:* The VCS, particularly in the form of smaller community-based organisations, has for some time been linked to the principle of 'community'. The explosion in research on social capital has given these debates empirical depth. Although less concerned with democratic participation and more focused on 'social' aspects of citizenship, theories and measures of social capital can help give debates about civil renewal empirical depth. They put research findings behind arguments designed to strengthen civil society, with evidence that when individuals associate with each other and engage in community affairs this can result in improved economic and social outcomes (see Performance and Innovation Unit, 2002 and Pattie *et al.*, 2002). The VCS should not just be thought of as an expression and measure of social capital, however. It also plays an important role in promoting social capital in local communities (we return to this below).

3   *Site for learning citizenship skills:* Although citizenship education, now part of the national curriculum, will go some way to teaching the habits of active citizenship, it is through 'doing' that most people learn. As Richard Dagger notes, in order to cultivate civic virtues, republican liberals want a thriving civil society (Dagger, 1997). VCOs provide key building blocks in civil society and important sites where citizens and communities can develop the skills required to be active citizens.

The VCS is important in achieving the civic society or civil renewal objectives that government ministers have expressed. It would ideally be possible to develop an increased service delivery role whilst retaining the qualities which enable the sector to contribute to the three areas listed above. However, there are tensions. A more professionalised VCS with closer (particularly contractual) relations with government may find that it erodes some of the very qualities which allow it to make such a distinct contribution to the vitality of civil society. Policy needs to focus more on policies which help ensure a strong VCS as part of stronger communities and wider civil society.

4 A BALANCED APPROACH

We have argued that current government policy does not sufficiently address how to harness the VCS as a vehicle for achieving civil renewal objectives. In this section we discuss the implications for thinking about how the state should relate to the VCS, and then we suggest some specific policy recommendations. We are not arguing that the VCS has no role to play in future public service reform. It does. Instead government policy needs to address two crucial issues more rigorously. First, how can the distinct added value that VCOs bring to public service provision, like increased levels of trust and better public participation, be protected and built upon? In other words, how can civil renewal and public service reform objectives be achieved simultaneously? Second, and more fundamentally, how can policy makers achieve a more appropriate balance between supporting the VCS merely as a potential or actual service provider and supporting it as an integral part of a strong civil society? Below we concentrate primarily on the second issue – if government policy were more focused on the role that the VCS can play in the context of civil society and civil renewal, then what might the impacts on policy be?

Developing local civic infrastructure

One implication is to think more broadly about how the state can relate to and influence the VCS. Contracts to provide services are only one type of relationship. The state can also promote local partnerships, for example with Local Strategic Partnerships, and provide grant funding and support for infrastructural investments Gaster and Deakin (1998, p. 3) have developed the concept of a 'ladder of partnership' as one way of understanding the different relationships between the VCS and government. It is also possible to think more strategically about the relationship between the VCS and the state. What forms of state structure are most conducive to enabling an active civil society and strong VCS?

Two points need making here. First, there is less evidence that the size of government affects the size of the voluntary sector than is often assumed. Although social policy historians often link the decline in traditional forms of welfare, such as friendly societies, to the introduction and expansion of national state-provided public services, there is relatively little evidence that 'bigger government' crowds out social capital and a strong civil society. Furthermore the state can potentially play an important enabling role. As Tony Wright and Andrew Gamble argued recently: 'in many respects the issue is not whether the state should be bigger or smaller, but how it can be smarter' (Wright and Gamble, 2004, p. 8).

Second, it is not just the size of the state which is relevant – the type of government is also important. The work of Lowndes and colleagues, as well as research by the LSE's Centre for Civil Society, suggests strongly that opportunities for associational life and VCS activity are created (or hampered) by the constitutional and legal structures of the state (Begum, 2003; Lowndes et al., 2002). Their work focuses on local government in the UK and it suggests that open structures or channels of communication can enable a strong VCS. Important aspects of the local 'civic infrastructure' that they identify include: 'support for co-ordinating bodies within civil society (like ... volunteer bureau) ... facilitating access to local politicians and managers; developing the skills and capacity of citizens and groups to make use of that access; "pooling" and/or arbitrating between diverse voices of citizens; and monitoring the response of decision makers to participation' (Lowndes *et al.*, 2002, p. 4). This is about a relationship between local government and the VCS, but not just one which is based on contracts.

Given politicians' desire not just to promote social capital but also wider civic and democratic participation, it is instructive that both the studies cited above draw a similar conclusion about how the state/VCS relationship encourages particular forms of citizen participation. The LSE work, for example, argues that social capital is more likely to be invested in formal activity and direct political participation in policies and decision-making of government where aspects of a local 'civic infrastructure' are in place and where the voluntary and community sector has a healthy relationship with the local authority (Begum, 2003).

The Compact between the VCS and government (at both a local and national level) seeks to enable such a positive relationship.[1] But it is unclear whether it has been developed with wider civil renewal objectives in mind, as opposed to being intended simply to manage the relationship between the VCS and government when they enter into contractual relationships (Craig *et al.*, 1999). Although the Codes of Practice that accompany the Compact offer a framework for consultation, it has not ensured that relations are always effective. In many parts of the country consultations are not about policy formation, but rather about examining the impact of already decided policy. The VCS involvement in local decision making needs to become the norm, not the exception.

Concluding remarks

In the short term, there is an important need for further work on the nature of a successful local 'civic architecture'. Local government in particular, but also central government, needs to be incentivised to engage constructively with the VCS. This could be achieved by considering radical changes to what is measured under the Comprehensive Performance Assessment (CPA), which is used by central government to assess which local authorities are doing well.

In the longer term, if policy makers are to achieve a balance between seeing the VCS as a possible service provider and as a contributor to the strength of communities and civil society, key existing policy objectives and targets may need to be revised. As part of the 2004 spending review the government reset the Public Service Agreement target relevant to the VCS. Home Office Public Service Agreement 6, element 2 aims to 'increase the voluntary and community sector contribution to delivering public services'.[2] The success criterion for this target is not hard to achieve – it will be met if 'the voluntary and community sector contribution to delivering public services is higher in 2007/08 than in the baseline period [2003/04]' (Select Committee on Home Affairs, 2005). Nevertheless these targets are important as they will shape civil service and government priorities and focus. At present there is a danger that the civil society aspect of debates about the VCS can be lost. For example, although the Home Office has established a Civil Renewal Unit it is doubtful whether it has significant clout.

Until this happens it is likely that the focus of government and, crucially, funding streams will continue to disproportionately favour developing the VCS with an eye to enabling it to deliver more public services. For example, while schemes like the Adventure Capital Fund, which aims to develop new models of sustainable funding for the sector, remain small, the Futurebuilders fund represents significant government spending. And this opens up the dangers this paper has highlighted: that government policy will undermine the very added value which the VCS has and its importance in a strong civil society. A more nuanced target could attempt to measure not just direct delivery of public services but the 'robustness' of the funding base and the support available for the sector as a whole.

It is right to challenge and reform the state. The need to match increasing public demands and to provide services which add 'public value' (by being accountable to citizens, providing services tailored to users' needs and increasing public trust) highlights the continued role that the VCS will play in public service reform. But at present it is questionable whether the balance struck between this objective and a civil renewal agenda is the right one. The state needs to find more and better ways of using VCS policy to develop the 'little platoons' upon which the strength of civil society rests.

NOTES

Chapter 2

1   See http://www.hm-treasury.gov.uk/media/890/03/
    CCRVolSec02.pdf for the first. The second is still to report at
    the time of writing.

2   See http://www.homeoffice.gov.uk/docs3/
    HomeOffice_SR04_TNs.pdf for further details of the precise
    PSA.

3   By 'earned income' we mean income derived from the sale
    of goods or services where a fee is paid by the recipient, or
    recipient's agent, although not necessarily at market value.
    By 'voluntary income' we mean income given freely for no
    commercial consideration, usually in the form of grants or
    donations.

Chapter 4

1   The Compact, signed in November 1998, codifies a mutually
    developed and reviewed framework for the working
    relationship between government and the VCS, and
    provides a resource against which to solve any conflicts and
    to determine behaviour. It has been applied to over 200 of

the 388 local authority areas. The government has issued a publication deadline of April 2005 for the remaining local authorities.

2   See http://www.homeoffice.gov.uk/docs3/ HomeOffice_SR04_TNs.pdf.

REFERENCES

Anheier, H.K. and Romo, F.P. (1992) 'The philanthropic transaction', paper presented at the 1992 Convention of the American Sociological Association, Pittsburgh, PA

Begum, H. (2003) *Social Capital in Action: Adding up Local Connections and Networks*. London: Centre for Civil Society, LSE

Billis, D. and Glennerster, H. (1998) 'Human services and the voluntary sector: towards a theory of comparative advantage', *Journal of Social Policy*, Vol. 27, No. 1, pp. 79–98

Blunkett, D. (2003) *Civil Renewal: A New Agenda*. London: Home Office

Bolton, M. (2003) *Voluntary Sector Added Value*. London: NCVO

Brown, G. (2004) 'Civic renewal in Britain', speech to NCVO. Available at http://www.hm-treasury.gov.uk/newsroom_and_speeches/press/2004/press_14_04.cfm

Craig, G., Taylor, M., Szanto, C. and Wilkinson, M. (1999) *Developing Local Compacts: Relationships Between Local Public Sector Bodies and the Voluntary and Community Sectors*. York: Joseph Rowntree Foundation/ York Publishing Services

Dagger, R. (1997) *Civic Virtues: Rights, Citizenship and Republican Liberalism*. Oxford: Oxford University Press

Dekker, P. and van den Broek, A. (1998) 'Civil society in comparative perspective: involvement in voluntary associations in North America and Western Europe', *Voluntas: International Journal of Voluntary and Nonprofit Organizations*, Vol. 9, No. 1, pp. 11–38

DiMaggio, P.J. and Powell, W. (1983) 'Institutional isomorphism and collective rationality in organization fields', *American Sociological Review*, Vol. 48, No. 2, pp. 147–60

Edwards, M. (2004) *Civil Society*. Cambridge: Polity Press

Gaster, L. and Deakin, N. (1998) 'Local government and the voluntary sector: who needs whom – why and what for?', paper presented at the Third International Conference of the International Society for Third-Sector Research, Geneva, 8–11 July

HM Treasury (2002) *The Role of the Voluntary and Community Sector in Service Delivery: A Cross Cutting Review.* London: HMSO

Jeavons, T. (1992) 'When management is the message: relating values to management practice in nonprofit organisations', *Nonprofit Management and Leadership*, Vol. 2, No. 4, pp. 403–17

Kelly, G. (2000) *The New Partnership Agenda.* London: IPPR

Kelly, G., Mulgan, G. and Muers, S. (2002) *Creating Public Value. An Analytical Framework for Public Service Reform.* Available at http://www.strategy.gov.uk/files/pdf/public_value2.pdf

Kendall, J. and Knapp, M. (1993) *Defining the Nonprofit Sector: The United Kingdom.* Working Papers of the Johns Hopkins Comparative Nonprofit Sector Project

Lowndes, V., Pratchett, L. and Stoker, G. (2002) 'Social capital and political participation: how do local institutions constrain or enable the mobilisation of social capital?', paper for the Robert Putnam Cambridge Social Capital Seminar, 19 November

Milburn, A. (2004) See http://www.acevo.org.uk/main/index.php?content=newsitem&news_id=47

NCVO (National Council for Voluntary Organisations) (2004) *The UK Voluntary Sector Almanac 2004.* London: NCVO

Pattie, C., Seyd, P. and Whiteley, P. (2002) 'Does good citizenship make a difference?', paper presented to EPOP Annual Conference, University of Salford. Available at http://www.shef.ac.uk/politics/citizenaudit/EPOP02.doc

Performance and Innovation Unit (now the Strategy Unit) (2002) *Social Capital: A Discussion Paper.* London: The Stationery Office. Available at http://www.number10.gov.uk/su/social%20capital/socialcapital.pdf

Petrella, F. (2001) 'Proximity services in Belgium', *Annals of Public and Cooperative Economics*, Vol. 72, No. 1, pp. 77–101

Pettit, P. (1997) *Republicanism: A Theory of Freedom and Government*, Oxford: Clarendon Press

Select Committee on Home Affairs (2005) *Third Report.* London: The Stationery Office. Available at http://www.publications.parliament.uk/pa/cm200405/cmselect/cmhaff/320/32014.htm

Tonkiss, F. and Passey, A. (1999) 'Trust, confidence and voluntary organisations: between values and institutions', *Sociology*, Vol. 33, No. 2, pp. 257–74

Wright, T. and Gamble, A. (2004) 'Introduction', in T. Wright and A. Gamble (eds) *Restating the State?* Oxford: Blackwell

Part II

Beyond transfer to transformation

Barriers and opportunities facing voluntary organisations providing public services

Julia Unwin and Peter Molyneux

1 BACKGROUND

Summary

In order to improve public service delivery, provide choice and fundamentally transform the relationship between the citizen and the provider of services, government has turned to the voluntary sector as agents for delivery. In response, some parts of the voluntary sector have responded enthusiastically, while arguing that the current environment makes it hard for them to play their full part. This paper argues that if this approach is to develop beyond a debate about simply technocratic solutions, and really effect transformative change, there will need to be both recognition of the preconditions that make such a transfer possible and a focus on overcoming the barriers which either inhibit transfer or minimise its impact.

Transfer will only work if it can build trust. Building trust requires a genuine transformation of relationships. If the transfer of services is to have an impact which is genuinely transformative – on service users, on commissioners of service and on the providers themselves – then two equally important outcomes are required:

- The services provided need to be better than the previous ones in ways which can be readily understood.

- The organisations providing the services need to demonstrate that they are sufficiently resilient to offer security of service.

continued

This paper examines the ways in which the process of transfer can be best managed to deliver effective, sustainable and transformative change.

It is informed by the experiences of a number of voluntary organisations, details of which are given in Appendix 3. Reference to these case studies will assist in clarifying the points made below.

Developing the role of the voluntary sector in the planning and delivery of public services is an objective for all the main political parties. They look to the voluntary sector to help deliver services for a range of reasons. In part they believe that a mixed economy of providers can offer greater consumer choice. They also consider that the voluntary sector offers a better breeding ground for innovative thinking about practice, and are persuaded that, again in some areas, the voluntary sector can offer greater community and local engagement or control. Equally they believe that some voluntary organisations have demonstrated that not only can they develop services to meet the needs of individual consumers, they can also offer the users the potential to lead and manage the services themselves. In a pluralist society, they argue, the voluntary sector can offer more appropriate, more user-responsive services.

For many voluntary organisations this is nothing new. Since their inception they have provided assistance to their users, working closely with the statutory authorities to provide a range of personalised interventions. From residential care to housing, childcare and child protection, as well as through the voluntary youth service, voluntary organisations have been centrally involved in providing services that are also delivered by the public sector. The community sector too, is no stranger to offering services.

Playgroups and youth clubs, visiting housebound older people and advocacy and advice sessions all have their roots in community-controlled local organisations.

The last decade, however, has witnessed a policy interest in expanding this contribution, and there have been a range of initiatives designed to encourage the transfer of services from the public sector to the voluntary sector. Some of these have been specifically designed to ensure greater plurality of provision and hence greater choice. Others have been in recognition of the more targeted provision that can be offered by the voluntary sector and others still have been designed to promote the community and user control of services.

2 BEYOND PUBLIC SERVICE

The debate about public service delivery has a number of different aspects. Of necessity, it is a dynamic debate in which the terms change as the different participants develop their thinking and interaction.

Until recently, the state's agenda was largely focused on the need to improve public service delivery, primarily through diversifying providers. This greater diversification would, it is argued, provide both individual service users and the purchasers acting on their behalf with choice. Choice in turn would enable a more personalised service and would also drive up quality through competition.

For the voluntary sector, the debate had focused much more on technical solutions to enable the market to operate effectively, and specifically to enable voluntary sector organisations to participate. Thus, there has been a focus on full cost recovery, the need for longer-term contracts and for a more appropriate, sector-sensitive, regulatory environment.

Today, the development of a market response is seen as one of a suite of mechanisms which can together drive cultural change. While the state still looks to the voluntary sector for diversification, it is also looking for an increased user focus. The challenge to the sector, then, is to develop solutions that are not simply user responsive, but user controlled and directed. Meanwhile, the voluntary sector is more clearly articulating the need to enhance voice and also provide choice.

Extending the range of choices available is just one of the ways in which the voluntary sector can contribute to building public value, not just as a high-volume provider of public services, but as an agent of civil renewal. While the technical issues that obstruct the operation of the market and cause difficulty for purchasers and providers alike are real and require resolution, the prize is a more dynamic, more responsive, effectively user-controlled set of services. Achievement of this prize requires a cultural transformation of public services which goes beyond the introduction and development of a market of providers.

For this reason, the ambition for the future is to develop a transformed relationship between the individual and the state. The networks and the organisations that can enable this to happen are found throughout civil society. Here transparency, accountability and legitimacy are as important as organisational structures.

The creation of services that build public value is challenging and difficult. It is based on three fundamentally changed relationships:

- between the individual citizen and the state

- between the voluntary sector and the individual citizen

- between the state and the voluntary sector.

To date, the agenda for discussing this has been either theoretical or technocratic. Changing these three relationships offers a way of developing and delivering public services that are genuinely transformative.

3 THE RESPONSE OF THE VOLUNTARY SECTOR

In this context, it is too easy to see the voluntary sector as simply a delivery arm, willing to provide public services if the contractual arrangements are right.

The reality is rather different. Most voluntary organisations have an interest in public service reform. Whether involved in direct service delivery, in civil renewal or in a wide range of other activities, they will have a role in amplifying the voice of the service user and will be keen to see the proper and planned development of high quality services. They will also know that service delivery alone is not enough. Without the development of strong, resilient and empowered communities, the intention of delivering better services will always be frustrated. Voluntary organisations operate within a complex ecology of services and activities. Strengthening the communities in which services operate, building communities that can cope and ensuring the development of the voice of the user are all equally important functions in the development of the reform and modernisation of the public services. So too are advocacy and scrutiny, and all the other processes that hold the providers of services to account.

A part of the voluntary sector is additionally willing to run services themselves. For these organisations there is a strategic choice. In determining whether or not they are willing to run the services that were previously largely managed and directed by the state, they will consider the extent to which this provision:

- helps the organisation meet its own mission

- will help beneficiaries

- is funded in a sustainable manner.

They will then need to determine whether or not they can run the particular service in a better and more responsive manner.

This analysis suggests that the agenda of public service reform and modernisation is of critical importance to the voluntary sector as a whole. The issue of transferring services to voluntary management and control will only be a priority concern for particular voluntary organisations.

4   THE OPERATING ENVIRONMENT

The voluntary sector operates across a very large number of fields. Each of these has its own specific operating environments, and the case studies we have selected reflect the very different circumstances facing, for example, voluntary sector providers of museums, community-based providers of transport and waste management, and the different organisations providing housing, health and social care. Inevitably, in each subsector significantly different circumstances influence the development of the organisations. There are, however, some general comments that frame the discussion.

Working with others

Voluntary organisations operating at local, regional and national level are part of a local ecology of organisations, groups and relationships. They do not and cannot operate as individual actors, making decisions separately. Indeed, for most voluntary organisations, their capacity and their authenticity depend in part on their relationship with others.

One set of these relationships is the business relationships that any organisation has. Voluntary organisations are members of co-ordinating bodies, some of which operate as trade organisations. Others operate in a standard-setting mode, while others have a significant policy development function. In these organisations, voluntary organisations are enabled to work together, and some of the terms of trade are established.

Voluntary organisations also have sets of working relationships with other organisations which are not part of the voluntary sector. Through the planning and commissioning processes of most local statutory agencies, voluntary organisations work closely with their colleagues in the statutory sector.

The interaction with organisations which exist to amplify the voice of the service user or carer will have a significant impact on the activity of a service-providing organisation. While organisations specifically established to advocate will have a carefully defined role, so too will the many organisations which engage in other ways in the development and monitoring of services.

The funding environment

The voluntary sector still operates in a revenue-based economy and is still largely supported by annual grants or contracts for services. Its planning horizons will therefore tend to be short-term, and most voluntary organisations do not have the funded capacity to think ahead and plan strategically. In complex negotiations with parts of the statutory sector that have both intellectual capital and planning flexibility, the sector will feel disadvantaged. Additionally, research and development monies must be transferred to the voluntary sector, many argue, if it is to play a proper role in the dovolopmont and reconfiguration of services.

The voluntary sector is also, at least in comparison with its private and statutory competitors, likely to be asset poor. A small minority of voluntary organisations own their own physical assets and the overwhelming majority have very little on their balance sheet. This on its own affects their ability to enter into a trading market. Their ability to borrow in anticipation of income is entirely circumscribed. Equally they have little flexibility with which they can prepare for changes in service delivery.

The voluntary sector brings expert knowledge, a degree of credibility with users and within the wider community, and an authority that flows from direct experience. Even so, many voluntary sector providers argue that they are seen as offering less than a statutory provider with an established overhead and strategic capacity. This is exacerbated by the lack of a democratic mandate within the voluntary sector and the sense that this limits both the credibility and the mandate of the voluntary organisation in any negotiation.

The regulatory environment

This sense of disadvantage is further compounded in the regulatory arrangements. All public services, delivered in any sector, are now subject to significant regulation and inspection. However, there are two particular issues for voluntary organisations:

1   *The choice of legal framework:* for charities the Charity Commission remains the regulator and will continue, if the Charities Bill is enacted, to have responsibility for the integrity of charity law. Charity law provides a double lock on assets and so, in theory at least, should be attractive for those seeking to transfer public services. The transfer can, with confidence, require the services and assets to be held in trust for the community in perpetuity.

    The development of Community Interest Companies, as alternative vehicles, is as yet untried but may provide another means by which organisations can be formed in order to take over these services.

2   *The role of the regulator in supporting transfer:* the Charity
    Commission's framework, while entirely compatible with
    any proposed transfer of public services, was not designed
    to manage significant asset transfers, and other regulators
    will need to develop a role in supporting or facilitating
    transfer if they are to become a regular feature of the
    market.

The Charity Commission will, however, remain neutral
about such a transfer, seeking to protect the charitable
framework and the integrity of the individual charity.
Similarly, the Commission for Social Care Inspection (CSCI
– which regulates the providers of personal social services,
in all sectors), is primarily concerned with the end-user
experience.

An asset lock is vital so we can't be demutualised.
                        (Hackney Community Transport)

Other regulators have had a role in shaping and enabling
the market to make transfer possible and, for the
complexity of transfer that this paper outlines, there will
need to be some clear regulatory support for the approach.

The Housing Corporation (the housing association regulator)
has adopted a different stance on this issue. It has
facilitated the transfer of large swathes of formerly
municipal housing to community control through the Large
Scale Voluntary Transfer programme. In doing so, it has
been guided by the government's own commitment to a
stock transfer programme, as well as a view that the new
financing opportunities provided through stock transfer are
a good way of bringing about the necessary improvement
in the condition of the stock.

The role of the Housing Corporation in enabling the transfer programme to take place is significant. While some of this was through its direct regulatory role, it also inevitably developed a store of knowledge and understanding about these issues, which means that new transfer propositions were built on previous experience and knowledge. Whether by design or coincidence, knowledge of models, approaches, pitfalls and opportunities was held centrally. This sort of knowledge management function was replicated at the National Housing Federation (the trade association for housing associations), and undoubtedly contributed to the viability of so many transfers, and the relative speed with which they took place.

Changes in the operating environment

The operating environment for all voluntary organisations involved in service provision is volatile and predictions are unreliable and difficult to make. One likely change may be heralded by the imminent Department of Health Green Paper. If speculation is correct and this document significantly boosts the use of Direct Payments, there will be a dramatic change in the environment for care organisations. While this will give users more control, and will introduce a much more obvious market system, it will also present real challenges to the business model currently employed. The current business model usually assumes a block contracting approach, in which commissioners are able to offer service providers some certainty of income. This picture may be very different in the future.

The development of Direct Payments is actually a very helpful paradigm of the dilemmas facing voluntary organisations in considering process. On the one hand, organisations that wish to put the service user much more centrally in charge of the development and delivery of services will welcome the development of Direct Payments and see them as a clear expression of user choice and control. On the other hand, the use of Direct Payments may, potentially, be destabilising to the business model as it can undermine security of demand. In order to compensate for this, provider organisations need to attend much more carefully to meeting the demands of their service users. They may also need more assistance in managing a business model with a volatile and changing demand base.

5 PRECONDITIONS OF SUCCESSFUL TRANSFER

What are the preconditions that make a transfer of services possible?

Through this study we have identified a number of preconditions that need to be met and issues that need to be addressed if the transfer is to be successful and deliver a change in user experience. These are set out under the following headings:

- drivers for transfer

- stakeholder attitudes

- business planning

- governance.

We consider these in relation to the case studies detailed in Appendix 3.

Drivers for transfer

In analysing the position of the statutory organisation and the recipient organisation, we have isolated a number of drivers which need to be in place before transfer, if such a change is to occur.

These can be summarised as market, service and financial drivers.

Market drivers

We have identified significant *market failure* as an important precondition. This might take the form of customer dissatisfaction and professional disengagement, perhaps evidenced in a desire to see new and different ways of operating. Thus, for example, it became clear to those proposing a new model for managing the museums service in York that the current system was not capable of generating sufficient income for business development.

> The momentum to go for Trust status came from the local authority. The confidence to go for Trust status came from the skills and competences of the Initiation Group and their ability to attract investment.
>
> (York Museums Trust)

The second significant market-based driver has been identified as the *absence of choice*. In the changes that led to the development of Yarrow Housing, for example, it was clear that the options provided by the health authority for the education and care of young people with learning difficulties were seen as simply too narrow and were unsatisfactory to the young people, their parents, and the professionals advising them. In this instance the existing system, whether market-based or not, was seen to have failed to offer sufficient choice.

Closely associated with this is *commissioner capacity and willingness to stimulate the market*. Where commissioners recognise the need to develop alternative providers, and have been able to invest in doing this, they are much more likely to facilitate a transfer. Commissioners who do not see this as part of their brief, viewing the market as purely neutral, will probably not engage in such a transfer. This was evident in our conversations with both THT (Terence Higgins Trust) Lighthouse and Yarrow Housing Association. In both of these examples, the willingness of those in positions of responsibility within the statutory sector to use market diversification to achieve modernisation made the two very different transfers possible. In all cases, the proposal either to create a charitable trust or to deploy an existing trust was critical in building support. All parties recognised that a charitable trust could behave like a public body accountable to stakeholders rather than a private organisation accountable to shareholders.

Had they seen no merit or advantage in using a transfer model as a means of improving service quality, there would have been little likelihood that it would take place. Commissioners who remain focused on improving the in-house service, or see the private sector as the only alternative provider, are unlikely to effect a transfer to the voluntary sector. However, when users and commissioners consider that there is market failure and commissioners consider that the voluntary sector offers real advantages, then there is likely to be scope for transfer.

Service drivers

The service drivers are often only an alternative form of expression for the market drivers. Thus, for example, the user or carer dissatisfaction that undoubtedly fuelled the decision to transfer housing from local authority control to voluntary sector control, through a Large Scale Voluntary Transfer, is also an example of market failure. Essentially, the market was unable to generate the sort of solutions that could satisfy the demands and requirements of tenants in those localities.

This is particularly clear where it is the *purchaser or commissioner expressing dissatisfaction.* In these cases, it is the statutory purchaser, acting on behalf of the individual client, who identifies a weakness in the current service configuration and seeks alternative providers. In the case of Yarrow Housing Association, there was a loss of confidence by the purchasers and care managers both in the configuration of care and the capacity of existing providers to deliver change, which encouraged them to look for alternative forms of delivery.

Financial drivers

The third set of drivers are financial. Where the proponents of change can identify alternative sources of finance, either as access to capital markets or through the development of alternative sources of income, including voluntary and charitable income, it acts as a driver. In those instances where significant, and reliable, *financial incentives* can be identified, it also seems easier to manage the process of transfer. These external incentives are not only financial. Those organisations operating in a market which has been consciously stimulated by the commissioners may find themselves more readily able to manage the risks associated with the possible transfer.

In the many cases where the financial imperative seems to be more uncertain, and indeed unreliable, then this presents a very significant barrier. This is particularly the case when organisations are considering a potential business model which might enable them to run a service. When the price paid seems inadequate, or the investment unpredictable, it is more difficult to get agreement.

In the case studies considered for this paper, the existence of all of these drivers seemed to be necessary for any significant transfer to take place.

Attitudes to transfer

Organisations wishing to transfer services need to attend to the attitudes and responses of a range of stakeholders. In doing so they need to recognise that these attitudes are not all the same. Anxiety about transfer will not necessarily be translated into formal objection. It may instead manifest itself as a profound lack of trust, unwillingness to co-operate and very high levels of anxiety. In other instances it can be a withdrawal of mandate, making it difficult for the negotiating bodies to operate effectively.

The *attitudes and responses of service users* are critical in determining the outcome. Where they favour a transfer, and can see positive change for themselves, they can be a major driver for change. At Yarrow Housing Association, for example, it was the enthusiasm and vision of some of the parents which facilitated the transfer discussion and eventual decision to invest in new services. Where they are concerned about the nature of the transfer, they represent a significant barrier to such a transfer taking place. This has been most clearly illustrated in the housing sector, where legislation provides the tenants of public housing with a veto on any transfer. In those localities where there has been an active 'no' campaign, tenants have frequently rejected the transfer proposition, even if the financial incentives seem to be clear and the dissatisfaction with existing provision is significant. It is, of course, only in the housing context that service users have the right to veto a proposed transfer and this gives them a very significant voice.

Equally important is the *capacity and attitude of the providers*. Some parts of the voluntary sector can be ambivalent about the transfer proposition, with many seeing it as either diversionary or too risky. Those that are more enthusiastic and view it as another means of delivering their mission, may nevertheless fear that their own capacity is too limited, particularly at the pre-transfer stage.

The second major group influencing the speed, direction and nature of the transfer are the staff. *Staff attitudes to transfer* were, in the cases we examined, critical to the approach taken. If those promoting the transfer have the choice between describing this as change or continuity, in the studies we considered, it seems to be the case that staff were presented with a vision of continuity.

> We didn't want staff to be anxious at all about leaving the 'mother ship'. Our intention was to make sure that the transfer date felt to them like any other working day, and we made a great deal of effort to ensure this.
> (Director, Yarrow Housing Association)

In order to deal with staff anxiety in all the cases, considerable effort went into ensuring that staff were not disadvantaged financially through the process of transfer and that basic systems were in place for payroll, pensions etc. The emphasis was on cultural change and the need to deliver a different end-user experience.

> Our drivers like the fact that all the profits are reinvested in the service.
> (Hackney Community Transport)

The third and final group with an interest, and ultimately control, are the *governors of the receiving charity or not-for-profit organisation*. As the custodians of the organisation receiving the service, they hold it in trust and will need to assess the risk of the proposed transfer of service. Where an existing organisation 'receives' the service, the governors of the existing organisation need to weigh up the costs and benefits of accepting the service. In particular, they will wish to consider the impact such a transfer will have on their existing service base and organisational priorities.

In practice, of course, the decisions are rarely that simple. While the governing body may well be able to identify benefits for service users, and indeed may have confidence that they can run services better and more appropriately, they will also have concerns about capacity and their remit to shape and determine the services differently. In three of the cases, board members expressed concerns when faced with moving beyond their 'traditional' service area or geographical area of operation.

The board will be conscious of the need to change or adapt their own membership. While in some cases this can be done in a way which strengthens capacity, in the examples considered here, it was common for the local authority, or another transferring organisation, to ask for seats on the board and so, by default, develop a stakeholder board for the organisation.

Business planning

The appetite for financial risk in these transfers is, understandably, limited. Although clear financial advantage and a business plan indicating viability did not guarantee agreement, they did seem to make it much more likely. Nonetheless, there were concerns about the nature and value of the assets to be transferred.

The first concern is *cost allocation*. Services formerly run within the public sector operated within a large organisation, with overheads that are frequently hidden. The issue of underfunded contracts is well documented. The same issues apply when a more complete transfer, rather than a contract, is envisaged. All concerned will be exercised about the ways in which costs will be apportioned and the relationship between the price and the cost of the service. While this issue has dominated the debate about contracting of services, it is of particular salience when the discussion is about a proposed transfer. In the preliminary discussions about such a transfer, assurances about the nature of the costs to be met, the treatment of surpluses and the acceptance of realistic overheads all contribute to the climate of trust.

> A key issue was whether the City Council was willing to provide sufficient funding for the management of change.
> (York Museums Trust)

Closely associated with this is the extent of *leverage* available. While commissioners of services may be very conscious of the degree of leverage, and indeed this may be a primary motivation, the confidence of the receiving organisation may be more limited. So, for example, expectations of greater charitable flows may influence the transferring authority. The operating charity will know that charitable funding is limited, and much less available for services that were previously located in the public sector. What is more, all operating charities will know how expensive fundraising can be, and will be reluctant to pursue additional charitable funds to meet costs associated with transfer or with running transferred services. The alternative form of leverage is access to the capital markets. While in some senses, this may be more straightforward, there is nevertheless a significant degree of risk involved for the recipient organisation, and overstatements of the potential for leverage can be as damaging to confidence as an understatement of revenue available.

> You have to be able to make a surplus to be able to drive the business forward.
>
> (Community Transport)

This question of *access to additional funds* is in any event a vexed one. The aspiration for a more entrepreneurial style of management, raising additional funds and combining existing funds in more imaginative ways, is easier to say than to do. It requires a degree of flexibility, capacity and regulatory freedom that most of the organisations studied here lacked. The development of new forms of commissioning may enable such approaches to be underwritten in the future, but at the time of reviewing the evidence, it seemed to us to be a heroic aspiration. Lack of confidence in the implementation of the aspiration is a major barrier to transfer.

> Much of the funding we secured would have been available to the local authority but we had the incentive and the drive to go out and secure it.
>
> (York Museums Trust)

In the case studies considered, while all could demonstrate the more entrepreneurial approach, most were acutely conscious that their lack of assets limited their capacity to develop and grow. The exception was Willow Park, where the transfer of a significant asset base that had increased in value had enabled considerable organisational growth.

Governance

There are two different approaches identified within the case studies considered here. In the first the services are transferred to an *existing organisation*. Hackney Community Transport and Yarrow Housing were pre-existing organisations and the board members of those organisations took a full part in the discussion about whether or not to accept the transfer of responsibilities. In others, such as Willow Park Housing Trust or York Museums Trust, a new organisation was created in order to run the new service. In the former, the services were transferred to a voluntary organisation which needs to demonstrate its capacity to manage. In the latter, the transfer is to the voluntary sector, and a new organisation is created in order to receive the service.

In both models the governing board needs to demonstrate its capacity. Confidence in the governance arrangements will be enormously influential on those determining the outcome of the transfer arrangements. At Hackney Community Transport the existing board changed composition in response to the receipt of major service contracts. The purpose of these changes was largely to demonstrate capacity and enhance apparent effectiveness in order to satisfy the local authority commissioners. At Yarrow a stakeholder board was created comprising parents, commissioners and local authority councillors. This was primarily to allow the various agencies to manage their risk and build confidence in the new service.

In the second model, in which a board is created for the purpose of running the newly transferred services, the discussion about risks and benefits to the existing organisation is clearly unnecessary. However, there is still a need to manage risk in the public interest and it is significant that both at Willow Park Housing Trust and York Museums Trust (YMT) a stakeholder board was created. At YMT, the appointment of local authority councillors as trustees provided assurance to the authority as custodian trustee that its interests would be protected. Over time, people have been recruited primarily for the contribution that they can bring to the good governance of the organisation.

> The commercial acumen of new board members (both from the private and public sectors) brought a good balance of public sector ethos and private sector robustness.
>
> (Yarrow Housing)

While the appointment of a stakeholder board is probably suitable for management of the transfer, there are real and well-documented difficulties for a stakeholder board in managing growth or development. Three of the organisations participating in this study have gone on to build a board that seeks to act in the public interest and holds the executive to account.

The role of *umbrella bodies and advocacy organisations* seems to have been particularly pertinent to the success of transfer. In those subsectors with well-developed and well-resourced umbrella bodies, such as the housing association sector, there was support, engagement and the ability to share good practice. The fact that the key umbrella organisation in this sector was also supportive of the notion of transfer also meant that it became a vehicle for engagement and support, not an obstacle. In others, the opposition of the relevant umbrella body, and specifically the opposition of significant advocacy organisations, was, and remained, an obstacle.

In some of the more successful transfers a *skilled intermediary* has been able to facilitate the transfer. It is striking, for example, that the Large Scale Voluntary Transfer to Willow Park was in part, facilitated by the active engagement of the regional office of the National Housing Federation which was in a position to guide and support, offering good experience based on a far wider pool of national organisations. The case for transfer of the museums service in York was developed by experienced and skilled volunteers and it is striking that experience and knowledge were held by the chief executive, who had already been part of a similar transfer in Sheffield.

The need for capacity to support receiving organisations through this process is a repeated theme in this study. While some, such as Hackney Community Transport, have managed with little external support, they seem to have generated their own internal capacity, largely through the scale and range of transfers. The fact that they now run a number of different services, previously managed by the local authority, has enabled them to generate the overhead required for negotiation. Even with this critical mass, however, they are still stretched very thinly and remain vulnerable. For some others, the attempt to contain the work of managing the transfer and subsequent relationships within the existing costs had proved impossible.

We won't bid for something unless we like the specification. We want to be able to offer the best price but we want to be able to offer quality as well.
(Community Transport)

6 RISK: IDENTIFICATION, ASSESSMENT AND MANAGEMENT

No structural change is risk free. There is great potential for better, more innovative, user-controlled services in resilient organisations. However, the risks in achieving this objective are necessarily equally great. Assessment, management and communication of these risks are an essential part of the transfer process. Commissioners, providers and service users as well as the wider community, all need to be actively engaged in this process.

The identification of risk in any transfer process is likely to identify the following large risk areas:

- risks in the process which will damage public trust

- risks in the service outcome – the risk that the resulting service is insufficiently improved to justify the upheaval

- risks in the business model – that the resulting organisation is insufficiently resilient to survive both the task and the environment it faces.

These large risks associated with the transfer of individual services are mirrored by the risks facing the transfer process as a whole, which also need to be addressed:

- the changes to the shape of the voluntary sector, if large voluntary organisations grow through the transfer process and squeeze out some of the smaller, more specialist or local organisations

- that changes to the structure and operation of voluntary organisations will be advocated in order to prepare them for operating in this market, and that this process will result in significant and damaging mission drift.

These two risks to the integrity and shape of the voluntary sector need to be put in the context of the eventual improved outcome for service users and for the public at large.

This paper has argued that, in order to generate the sort of public trust that is required for a properly transformative approach to public services, the improvement of services and the development of resilient business models are key. These same requirements are faced in any analysis of risk.

Process risk

There are risks during the process of transfer, and the way in which they are handled can affect the outcome. The temptation for advocates of any transfer is to take an overly aggressive approach to promoting the transfer and in so doing, ignore the real concerns and anxieties of those involved, including users and sometimes their carers, staff and volunteers and partner organisations of all sorts. Unless these key partners are properly engaged in the process and enabled to understand the benefits of the approach through an articulated and compelling vision, it is probable that at some stage in the transfer process, their actions will disrupt the plans.

Therefore, the first step in managing the process risk requires the development of a shared understanding of direction and a common commitment to the vision. This is challenging, as these case studies have illustrated, and frequently the messages given to different stakeholders will differ in perceptible ways. Specifically, there is a temptation to describe the process of transfer to staff as a purely technical fix, while describing the impact as entirely transformative to service users. This mixed and contradictory message presents a very real risk for the transfer process.

A second element of process risk management requires fine judgement. In most transfers there are inevitably issues of commercial confidence and competition. There is therefore pressure to manage this process through a tightly controlled and largely secretive approach. However, the complexity of the service environment makes this extremely difficult. The involvement of a wide range of stakeholders, along with second-tier organisations, advocacy bodies and representatives of the wider community, is required if these organisations are fully to understand the nature of the transfer process and the potentially great prize. Although the involvement of these bodies in itself represents a risk to the process of transfer, without their involvement they can, by default, effectively attract the power of veto.

The involvement of stakeholders, using a wide and inclusive definition of the term, will go some way to ensuring that the transfer proposition is properly and thoroughly debated and that the development of the proposition takes place in a positive climate. There are other aspects to this process too. There is a fear within the local voluntary sector that transfer actually results in the strengthening of large national voluntary organisations at the expense of their better-connected, and potentially more capable, local counterparts. The examples looked at in this paper suggest that actually there is considerable scope for local organisations to play a part in transforming public services through the transfer route, but any transfer process needs to be open to local influence and ensure that the local organisations recognise the role they might be able to play.

A third and final element in the management of risk concerns the motivation behind the transfer. If all parties believe that they are genuinely acting of their own volition, and have considerable choice in the approach they take, their commitment to the process and to the outcome will be much greater. It is clear that, in particular, where local authorities believe that they are under direction to transfer services the mandate for the process is very much weakened.

Service risk

The risk that the service will not be transformed, or at least significantly improved, is a major one. Without such a marked – and recognised – improvement there is a risk that the costs, in every sense, of the transfer will have been simply disproportionate.

In part, this will be mitigated by a thorough and credible assessment of the potential for service improvement. When this is done properly, it can provide an effective vision. It can shape the direction of the newly transferred services and can set clear parameters for growth. However, this will only ever be partial. As this paper has demonstrated, most service improvement springs directly from the new governance and managerial arrangements and the ability of the new organisation to take risks and manage priorities differently. Nevertheless, there are ways in which the risk of service failure or, more properly, service inadequacy can be managed. These include the articulation of vision and the resulting framework for delivery. They also include the nature of the service planning, the successful recruitment of staff who are able to operate differently and the establishment of managerial structures that offer sufficient continuity to protect the services, while at the same facilitating a more entrepreneurial and innovative approach to service planning and delivery.

Business risk

Public services operate in a volatile environment. The introduction of market mechanisms, and the increasing determination to put service users in the position of purchasers, increases this volatility. Using independent, free-standing and frequently small organisations to deliver services in this volatile environment inevitably increases the risk. The business model under which transfers take place is, at best, immature and is certainly under-resourced. Under these circumstances it is not surprising that business risk is one of the three big areas of risk.

There are ways in which this can be mitigated. A careful and rigorous approach to cost allocation, pricing and contractual arrangements provides some assurance. So too does a measure of asset transfer, properly accounted for and managed. Investment in building the business capacity of the recipient organisations is still not the norm, and yet the skill base of the voluntary sector, in terms of business management, is well recognised. While some of the services available to support small businesses have been used to benefit voluntary organisations which are thinking of taking on these functions, this is by no means universal, and there are few examples of business support mechanisms tailored to organisations in this field.

Risk to the voluntary sector

This paper has argued that the whole voluntary sector has an interest in the public service reform agenda, while some individual organisations will have an interest in the transfer of services and activities. In analysing the risk, it needs to be noted that the widespread engagement of the voluntary sector in the delivery of public services does present the sector as a whole with some risks.

The organic growth of the sector, responding to demand and opportunity, has inevitably resulted in a patchy network of organisations. This does not, and cannot, provide consistency or equity. It does, however, allow for some highly responsive and connected services. If there is a substantial transfer, there must be a real risk that the delivery of high-profile services will alter the relationship between the voluntary sector as a whole and the general community, as well as the relationship between service user and provider. Each individual voluntary organisation will need to determine their own response, but for the leaders of the wider voluntary sector there are risks in this process which require management and mitigation. In particular the role of advocacy organisations, in their role of supporting individuals, will need protection and enhancement, if the sector is not to become overly identified with the role of provision.

However, this risk is, as yet, a remote one. The transfer of services is still only at a very early stage, and there is little evidence to suggest that the transfer process will achieve such a volume as to present a real and present threat.

7 THE IMPACT OF TRANSFER

In the cases studied there was a tension between:

- the vision of change and transformation and the vision of continuity and consistency

- the development of an entrepreneurial approach to financing the change and the requirement for secure financial and organisational underpinning.

   The transfer decision requires the intelligent management of these tensions. In the case studies we considered, it was possible to agree a transfer if:

- the financing arrangements allowed for sufficient confidence

- the regulatory environment permitted it

- there was sufficient capacity to facilitate the voluntary organisation either through internal capacity or through an intermediary or infrastructure organisation.

   When these three aspects were in place it then became possible for the transfer to take place. The way in which these were negotiated and the outcome of those negotiations determined whether the transfer was primarily a transfer of engagements or actually delivered a transformative response. The impacts on both the services and the organisations are considered below.

Impact on services

One measure of the impact on the service is the *development or amplification of voice* for service users. Another is the extent to which other forms of engagement are developed. In order to convince service users and the surrounding community that the transfer has enabled a transformation to take place, there need to be high expectations for this enhanced voice and new engagement. In all the transfers that considered they had achieved significant change, there was evidence of this. This amplification of voice provided an important form of *evidence* for the organisation and contributed significantly to the mandate for new service configuration and the *degree of choice* available to users.

For example, the changes described at Yarrow, and in particular the significant change to service configuration, was made possible because of the role of the service users in the organisation and their growing sense of ownership and engagement. In one sense this is simply the amplification of a user voice, but it is also illustrated by the alternative forms of engagement with service users and with the local community. This same amplification can be seen at Willow Park and at York Museums Trust where the changes brought about through transfer, while risky and difficult, do seem to have resulted in significant measurable change in terms of *user satisfaction*.

The extent of this cultural change can be overstated. There are few reliable measurements for determining either the extent of cultural change or the degree to which such cultural change affects the experience of service users. It is striking that few transfer agreements, or service-level agreements, specify customer satisfaction as a reportable measure, and yet the motivation for such changed management arrangements is nearly always found in a desire to change the customer experience. Examples of transfers which have replicated the previous management do exist, but for the experience to be transformative for service users there does need to be a significant cultural shift.

> Willow Park has been successful in combining the performance driven culture of the local authority and the customer focus of the voluntary sector.
>
> (Park Housing Trust)

Proponents of the role of voluntary organisations in the delivery of services previously managed in the public sector, refer to the importance of developing *social capital* as an example of the added value contributed by the sector. In one sense, this is another way of describing the cultural change to which service users and the community contribute. Measurement of such increased social capital is hard to find, although possible to identify. The capacity of Willow Park to create employment programmes and involve residents in crime reduction initiatives is evidence of enhanced social capital and would have been much more difficult for a municipal housing department to manage.

It seems likely that the change in the control of the organisation allows for different forms of behaviour within the organisation. While the rhetoric of public service delivery has tended to focus on the impact and outcomes, the experience of transfer actually suggests that the change in ownership, normally seen as simply a process question, is actually of critical importance. While the mandate must be to achieve better outcomes, it may be that the process of change actually creates an environment which is more ready and able to deliver these outcomes.

Impact on the organisation

In the most successful transfers, the provider organisations, with an enhanced role, changed their remit and their mandate in significant ways. In one example, Yarrow Housing, the transfer enabled a complete reconfiguration of services, because the transfer had, in effect, transformed not only the service but the organisation as well. It became the manager of responsive services for residents and their capacity to drive the new service configuration changed the way in which the organisation operated in the market.

The same was true of Hackney Community Transport. The transfer of significant services from the local authority to the community organisation meant that the organisation changed in its attitudes and in its style. It recognised the strength of its market position, and this gave it both enhanced stature and the ability to negotiate as an equal with both the statutory and private sectors.

While the appointment of a stakeholder board is probably suitable for management of the transfer, there are real and well-documented difficulties for a stakeholder board in managing growth or development. Three of the organisations participating in this study have gone on to build a board that is a public interest board, with the specific purpose of improving the *robustness of the organisation's governance*.

The operating environment will also shape the outcomes of transfer in other ways. While recruitment and retention are a major issue for the public sector, there is little evidence that the voluntary sector providers find it easier to recruit. Although in some particular community-based providers there may be a new pool of potential staff and volunteers, the nature of the transfer does not normally seem to affect the ability to recruit and retain staff. Indeed for some organisations, the smaller size, and hence the more limited promotion prospects, may be a possible disincentive. In assessing the extent to which the transfer has been a success, the extent to which the staff continue to be attracted to work is clearly an important measure of *organisational sustainability*.

A critical feature of the post-transfer environment is the resilience, or otherwise, of the funding framework. In the case studies we considered, it is clear that the new *funding ratios* enable the organisations to act in a more entrepreneurial manner. In most cases they have, in one way or another, been able to access other sources of funding, and have done so with considerable energy and ingenuity. However, most of them consider that the business model in which they are operating is insufficiently resilient for the purpose. Critically, they have still not been able to generate sufficient funds to enable them to plan ahead realistically or to take opportunities as they arise. In that sense they are in the same position as the former managers of the service. This similarity, however, cramps the new entity and limits its potential to be transformative.

In particular, the similar funding conditions and restraints may restrict the ability of the new organisation to address questions of culture as effectively as they might. More critically, it will inhibit the ongoing development of a user-responsive service to one which is user directed in some way or another.

The resilience of the business model has another aspect to it. For all but one of the services considered, the transfer that took place was a transfer of staff, skills and services. It was only at Willow Park that the capital asset was also transferred. It is therefore only Willow Park which presents a different sort of balance sheet and therefore a fundamentally different business model. While the other organisations considered had not argued for a transfer of the assets, the fact that this had not happened has reduced their strength as businesses, and this may in turn have affected their ability to make the other changes deemed necessary for transformation.

The successful service transfers examined in this study had been able to create a vision for the transferred service, achieving the active support and engagement of service users and their representatives. In doing this, those promoting the transfer need to deliver a complex, multilayered and frequently difficult message. While describing the benefits and the transformative potential of the transfer, they need to also provide reassurance about continuity and sustainability. These apparently mixed messages are both difficult to deliver and hard to hear. In the interests of demonstrating change, organisations frequently invest heavily in the external profile of the organisation, changing its logo, its livery and many of its external manifestations. In order to demonstrate continuity and sustainability, organisations will emphasise proximity, familiarity and the security of the known. The tension between these two presentations of change forms a critical part of the transfer process.

8 THE ROLE OF ASSET TRANSFER

The transfer of assets from municipal control to the voluntary sector is a long-standing issue for the voluntary sector. While the biggest single transfer has been the transfer of housing, the much smaller-scale transfer which is at the heart of the development trusts movement should also be acknowledged.

A transfer of physical assets can be very positive for the recipient organisation. It strengthens the balance sheet and can provide the organisation with a degree of security, as well as leverage to enable access to finance. As has been demonstrated in the areas where it has taken place, the receipt of a significant asset can enable the organisation to develop in ways that would never have been possible without the transfer.

However, the voluntary sector also has long experience of transferred assets that became, effectively, a major liability. Some of the University Settlements, for example, endowed in the nineteenth century, now have responsibility for buildings which are an expensive and not necessarily appropriate drain on the organisations' resources. Transferring buildings which are no longer useful and expensive to maintain, transfers liabilities and not assets.

There are other assets, however, which are less clearly evident on a balance sheet. Voluntary organisations hold significant assets in terms of local credibility and support. They may have considerable expertise and skill in the area. Additionally they may be contributing an asset of volunteer help and charitable funding.

The statutory transferring authorities will also have assets. These may be held in the form of skilled and experienced staff, research and development capacity and democratic legitimacy.

Balancing these assets, and ensuring that they are appropriately valued, can make explicit the very real contribution being made by both the voluntary organisations and the transferring authority. A transparent accounting framework which is able to focus attention on the less tangible assets that are under consideration, will contribute to the public trust in the process that this paper has argued, is central to making transfer of services a genuinely transformative process.

9   THE QUESTION OF CAPACITY

Much of the current drive for transfer, whatever the motivation, assumes the existence of capacity:

- within the voluntary sector to take on services

- among commissioners and purchasers to plan effectively

- among service users to ensure their voice is properly heard.

It is clear that in each of these areas capacity is extremely limited. The existence of voluntary organisations able and willing to engage in these discussions is in itself limited. In some parts of the country and for some public services, there are simply very few voluntary organisations in existence. Those that do exist are frequently locked in a cycle of raising funds simply to keep going and may not have the intellectual and managerial capacity to engage with a transfer proposition.

This limited capacity is by no means confined to the voluntary sector. Statutory organisations also require particular strategic, managerial and business skills to effect a transfer and these are frequently lacking. What is more, they consider transfer in an increasingly febrile and fast-changing political environment, and officials and members alike need the skills to manage the complex agenda of transfer.

Developing a clear, powerful and effective voice for service users is also complex, and is frequently a requirement, either on the same voluntary organisations as are called on to deliver service or on organisations which are equally and similarly constrained.

Given these limits to capacity it is surprising that transfer takes place at all. In the cases we considered, there seem to be a number of compensatory factors that have enabled such a transfer to take place despite the limits on capacity.

- The existence of knowledge and experience inside one key individual. This was strikingly the case in York where the transfer of the museum was led by a director who had had earlier experience in managing such a transfer in another locality.

- The strength of a trade association able to hold knowledge and experience, and ensure that it was properly shared. This avoided the need to start every process from scratch in the Willow Park transfer.

- In the same example, the role of the regulator as advocate for transfer illustrated the way in which regulation could, unusually, facilitate the process of change.

- In some of the other examples it did seem to be the case that chance had inevitably played its part. The fact that some key people were in post at the time of the proposed transfer, undoubtedly affected the outcome in both Hackney and Yarrow, but without the skills, abilities and commitments of these individuals, it is unlikely that these transfers would have taken place.

It is striking that investment in capacity to enable this transfer process to take place is still embryonic. While the development of Futurebuilders as a resource to build capacity for public service delivery is acknowledged, there is little else in the environment designed to build capacity within all the actors.

10 TRANSFER OR TRANSFORMATION?

In making an assessment about the extent to which the transfer process has achieved the objectives of transformation, it is apparent that a key precondition for success is the existence of *public trust* and *confidence*. We observe there to be two dimensions to this question:

1   Those who are accountable to the public and who are asked to transfer services need to assess and manage risk on behalf of the public. Health service commissioners, local authority elected members and government ministers need assurance that the organisation to which they are proposing to transfer key services is credible.

2   The public need to have confidence that the proposition is one they can trust.

Measuring levels of trust is notoriously difficult. There are some principles that contribute to trust in terms of (i) *probity* in terms of adopting transparent and recognisable standards of audit and propriety; (ii) *sustainability* (as opposed to survivability) as there are real concerns about transferring important services to organisations with an uncertain or precarious future; and (iii) *consistency* and, as far as possible, equity.

However, there is a risk of simple assertion without evidence. In order to provide more reliable assessment, this report considers that both dimensions of public confidence and trust will only be developed where the organisation receiving the service has a focus on (i) *quality of service* and (ii) *resilience of the organisation*. For each of these objectives we propose a range of indicators.

Quality of service

In determining the extent to which quality is achieved there will be three primary measures:

- the *evidence base for action*, meaning the extent to which the provider organisation is basing intervention and activity on well-founded evidence, rather than precedent and past practice

- the *degree of choice* provided, meaning the extent to which service users are enabled not just to choose the nature of the provider, but are able to exert effective and meaningful choice about the services they receive from any one provider

- the evidence of *user or carer satisfaction*, which needs to be available to underpin any judgement about impact in this area.

The development of reliable indicators for each of these will be part of any assessment of quality of service.

Resilience of the organisation

The organisations taking on the delivery of public services need to be able to demonstrate that they are robust, well-managed organisations that can cope with the responsibilities they have taken on. The organisation will only be strong and resilient if it is operating on a sound business model. In determining the viability of the business model there will be three major measures of success:

- the *robustness of governance* and management, and the ability of the organisation to plan for a potentially uncertain future

- *funding ratios*, and in particular the relationship between borrowings and earnings, and the balance between earned and donated income

- the *number of purchasers* and the capacity of the organisation to balance their conflicting demands and cover the associated overhead costs.

Taken together, these six service and business indicators provide a means of assessing the extent to which the objectives of the transfer have been met and, at the same time, the capacity of these changes to be transformative. In considering the four organisations interviewed as part of this study and comparing them against these measures, a number of conclusions can be drawn.

Improvements to service

In each case the organisations concerned can point to significant changes in the nature and direction of the service offered. This was made possible in the Yarrow case by a new relationship with the carers and users of the service. In the new organisation the service users, and specifically the parents, developed the capacity to drive the organisation and shape it around their needs and requirements. Putting the user at the centre of services was enabled by the new organisational form. This resulted in a radically altered pattern of service, which is both more responsive to users and, increasingly, controlled and directed by the users.

In the York Museums Trust, a more entrepreneurial style of management enabled the development of more responsive services targeted at particular groups of customers and the development of new relationships. In Willow Park the injection of additional finance, as well as rising land values, gave the new organisation the opportunity to respond to the needs and aspirations of tenants. By providing the organisation with the money with which to improve the physical housing stock, the transfer also enabled the organisation to invest in building community support and renewal activities within the neighbourhoods. Hackney Community Transport has topped the quality of service league table for mainstream public bus routes in London, which is a source of pride to users and staff.

If all four have demonstrated a changed relationship with their service users, they can also point to some change in levels of satisfaction. There is evidence from each very different organisation that the change in control, combined with some significant internal managerial and cultural change, provides more choice and a different experience for service users and their advocates.

Quality of the organisation

All four organisations had taken steps to ensure that their governance arrangements were stronger, and in particular, were more acceptable to those proposing to transfer the service. One approach used to strengthen the boards was to adopt a form of stakeholder representation. This clearly provided all stakeholders with a degree of comfort during the transfer process. However, there are inevitably weaknesses in stakeholder governance and these may become more evident in the next phase. Specifically, the handling of conflicts of interest and the management of growth are issues that may bedevil boards that are primarily stakeholder representatives. Certainly, in terms of developing a sound business base, the boards created to facilitate the transfer may not be the most appropriate ones for managing the long-term business.

In other respects also, steps were taken by all the case study organisations to strengthen their management capacity. In some this was conducted through a transfer of managerial staff. They then faced the challenge of working in a new and rather more entrepreneurial culture, and became engaged in the process of constructing an organisation that looked different and behaved differently, while at the same time providing assurance of continuity.

Measurement of organisational strength in terms of financial viability raises different challenges. The most common approaches to measurement of financial robustness, including the degree of gearing within the finances and the balance sheet strength, are important but do not necessarily give the total picture. In only one example was there a transfer of the physical assets from the statutory sector to the voluntary sector. In Willow Park, where this happened, the balance sheet position of the organisation was transformed and this had significant impacts for its internal strength. Specifically, the changed balance sheet provided it with financial leverage and the capacity for independent action, which was lacking in the others.

On the other hand, the ability to form funding relationships with a wider range of organisations, even on a revenue-only basis, strengthens the capacity of an organisation. The York Museums Trust was able to work across the local authority and the regeneration bodies in the city and in the north of England to generate a range of income streams. While complex and costly to manage, the existence of different forms of funding provides some essential underpinning that can result, in the longer term, in a viable business.

In order to improve public service delivery, provide choice and fundamentally transform the relationship between the citizen and the provider of service, government has turned to the voluntary sector as agents for delivery. For this study, we have divided the issue into one of public trust and confidence necessary to allow the transfer, and the broader confidence required for continuing success. In the cases we considered there was clearly sufficient trust to enable the transfer to take place. However, as this report demonstrates, the absence of public trust does not of itself lead to a decision to transfer to the voluntary sector. There are instead a number of other responses that may be considered. The decision to use the voluntary sector, as opposed to a private provider, seems to be based in part on an estimation of the confidence that will be generated by the provider being not for profit and in part on the lack of confidence in the previous model. The description of 'market failure' frequently attributed to transfer propositions, may actually be better expressed as the dissipation of public confidence in what went before. Quality of service and quality of organisation are key, if we are to go beyond transfer to be transformative in the way envisaged.

11 Conclusions

There are a number of very different reasons for considering the transfer of services from municipal or statutory control to the voluntary or community sector. The opportunity to develop more innovative organisations, able to respond entrepreneurially to the challenges ahead of them, is a strong argument for transfer. So too is the chance to shape services around the needs and desires of service users. Transferring services can result in a more competitive market, in which the needs of users for high quality services can really drive performance.

However, the prize is much greater than simply better services, desirable though that would be. It is possible for transfer of services to sit at the heart of an approach that is truly transformative, enabling the radical reshaping of the relationship between the provider, the user and the whole community. Such a radical reshaping has the potential to really build trust. This paper has argued that in order for trust to be built:

- The service has to be significantly improved in ways that are recognised by all.

- The organisation running the services has to be robust and resilient.

Without these two conditions, there is little likelihood of trust being improved.

In order to improve services and develop strong organisations, the voluntary sector needs a new way of measuring change. It needs to be able to demonstrate to all stakeholders and to the public that it can really improve services, and most importantly that the organisation that is providing the services can be relied upon for the long term. Without these assurances the transfer will simply be seen as a change in label, not a change in reality.

It is also of critical importance that the capacity of the sector, the commissioners and the service users, is built. In order to do this, and to make the respective contributions clear, it is important for assets to be properly transferred, and for a wide definition of such assets to be adopted.

Changing the pattern of public service delivery is important in order to build public trust. For some voluntary organisations there are real advantages in agreeing to manage public services. Such a role can contribute to their mission, can deliver demonstrably better services to their beneficiaries and can be done in a sustainable and secure way. For these organisations, it is important that the processes and structures enabling transfers operate in such a way as to result in better services and more resilient organisations. For the health of the voluntary sector and the level of trust in public services, these changes are essential.

APPENDIX 1: PURPOSE OF THE PAPER

This discussion paper has been commissioned by the Joseph Rowntree Foundation to examine the ways in which such transfers of service can be effected, and in particular to consider the ways in which the impact of such a transfer can be truly transformative for the service user. The paper therefore does not consider the motivation or the desirability of transfer. Rather it focuses on the practical measures that could be taken to ensure that the aspiration of user-focused voluntary sector delivery can become a reality. In doing so, the paper seeks to identify the processes and preconditions which make such a transfer not just a viable proposition, but genuinely transformative. It does so by tracking the progress of four transfers of services, and asks the questions:

1 Were these transfers truly transformative?

2 And if not, what would have enabled them to be so?

It argues for a new approach to the transfer of services, away from simply subcontracting, to a fundamental transfer of assets.

Methodology

A series of semi-structured interviews were carried out with key stakeholders (a list of those interviewed is attached in Appendix

2). The interviews sought to gather data of stakeholders' views on the extent to which they identify transformation as an issue, what they perceive the key drivers to be and where they thought the greatest opportunity for change lies. Key issues explored were:

- the attitudes of different stakeholders and particularly users, to transfer

- the barriers to transfer and what losses are identified by voluntary organisations considering entry into these markets

- what are the key attributes that command trust

- the preconditions for such a change

- what changes to the regulatory or inspection framework are needed.

Four case studies from distinct areas of voluntary sector activity were produced. The intention is to demonstrate both the features that made such a transfer possible and the changes that would be needed to encourage further activity. Two case studies were selected from sectors where there is already considerable evidence of change, and two sectors where there appears to be potential but in which to date, there seems to have been little transfer.

Definitions

In order to examine this issue properly, it has been important to establish some parameters for the discussion and these can most easily be expressed through a series of definitions which inform the paper.

For this reason, the paper focuses on the *voluntary sector*, and embraces in this definition charitable organisations, community-based organisations, social enterprises, not-for-profit companies, embryonic community interest companies and Industrial and Provident Societies. It considers the *public services* which are either providing personal services to individuals, or those of general public benefit aimed at the wider public, but specifically excludes consideration of enforcement or regulatory services. Finally, it adopts a definition of *transfer* which includes the transfer of the management and ownership of the service from public control to voluntary management. It does not concentrate on the purely subcontractual work which is part and parcel of the work of many voluntary organisations but essentially involves the voluntary organisation in a supplier relationship.

Appendix 2: List of those interviewed as part of this project

Stakeholders

Harry Cayton	Department of Health
Dame Denise Platt	Commission for Social Care Inspection
Jim Coulter	National Housing Federation
Lord Adebowale	Turning Point
Stuart Etherington	NCVO
Dame Gill Morgan	NHS Confederation

Case studies

Mervyn Jones	Willow Park Housing Trust
Barbara Forshaw	Willow Park Housing Trust
Irene Lawrence	Willow Park Housing Trust
Janet Barnes	York Museums Trust
Robin Guthrie	York Museums Trust
Mike Woodhead	York Museums Trust
Tim Hughes	Yarrow Housing
Lindy Shufflebotham	Yarrow Housing
Diana Cadogan	Yarrow Housing
Dai Powell	Hackney Community Transport
Paul Ward	THT Lighthouse
Nick Partridge	THT Lighthouse
Andrew Ridley	Guy's and St Thomas' NHS Foundation Trust

List of attendees at Joseph Rowntree Foundation-convened seminar to discuss the issue

Lord Victor Adebowale, CBE
Chief Executive
Turning Point

Lord Richard Best
Director
Joseph Rowntree Foundation

Ann Blackmore
Head of Policy
NCVO

Stephen Bubb
Chief Executive
ACEVO

David Carrington
Independent Consultant

Jim Coulter
Chief Executive
National Housing Federation

Professor Nicholas Deakin
London School of Economics

Nicholas Doyle
Practical Environment

Roger Howard
Chief Executive
Crime Concern

Tim Hughes
Chief Executive
Yarrow Housing Limited

Maggie Jones
Policy and Practice
Development Manager
Joseph Rowntree Foundation

Peter Molyneux
Independent Consultant

Nick Partridge
Chief Executive
THT Lighthouse

Will Paxton
Research Fellow, Social Policy
IPPR

Nick Pearce
Acting Director
Institute for Public Policy
Research

Paula Ridley
Director
Calouste Gulbenkian
Foundation

Dr Duncan Scott
Research Fellow
Manchester University

Jane Steele
Office for Public Management

Clare Thomas
Chief Grants Officer
Bridge House Estates Trust
Fund

Julia Unwin
Independent Consultant

Dai Powell
Director
Hackney Community Transport

Campbell Robb
NCVO

Lindy Shufflebotham
Deputy Director
Yarrow Housing Ltd

Professor Marilyn Taylor
Professor of Urban
Governance and Regeneration
University of the West of
England

Clare Tickell
Chief Executive
NCH

Paul Ward
Deputy Chief Executive
THT Lighthouse

Appendix 3: Case studies

Hackney Community Transport

Hackney Community Transport (HCT) was set up in 1982 to provide transport options for people who are unable to access mainstream public transport. A portfolio of schemes includes a door-to-door transport service for people with mobility problems and a network of local 'Plus Buses' which link deprived areas with local services (shops, clinic etc.) and which run mainstream bus routes under contract.

Former nature of provision

The introduction in 1985 of franchise-operated bus routes, on five-year contracts, fundamentally changed the nature of the public transport market. At this time HCT, in common with other community transport organisations, was operating a small fleet of minibuses for hire by voluntary and community groups. The early 1990s saw the addition of employment schemes, accessible fixed-route services (Plus Buses) and a volunteer car scheme as well as traditional group transport. In 2001, HCT secured the contract to run the North East London Mobility Bus Service for Transport for London (TfL).

Drivers for change

HCT started as a group travel service for community and voluntary groups. There was an increasing recognition that there were large numbers of people who were excluded from services because of poor access to affordable transport options.

For example, HCT identified that many of the volunteers who drove the minibuses were unemployed. HCT put ten volunteers through professional driving courses and each of them went on to find full-time jobs with the company.

Attitudes to transfer

The traditional users of the service were the community groups who hired minibuses from HCT. Many of them expressed concern at plans to diversify activity and move away from local authority funding. However, the majority wanted the organisation to expand. Staff and unions also expressed concern at the transfer of services into HCT. However, this shifted over time as, first, unions saw their membership levels increase when services transferred into HCT and, second, staff increasingly appreciated that surpluses generated are reinvested in service.

Business planning

There was much discussion about how the organisation could stay locally relevant and develop the capacity necessary to offer a broad range of services, diversify its funding base and expand as a business. By 1990, HCT employed eight staff and by 1993 it employed 13 staff. Through this period of relatively modest expansion, the organisation clarified its desire to be opportunity driven, provided that the specification allowed for a quality service to be delivered. The successful delivery of the North East London

Mobility Bus Service for Transport for London (TfL) gave the organisation confidence to bid for a mainstream commercial bus service.

Up until 2003, the board comprised 15 people elected from the membership with two co-optees – an accountant and lawyer. It was this board that had agreed to the change of strategic direction. The move into the provision of mainstream bus routes triggered a review of governance and the move from a stakeholder board to a public interest board. The board now comprises one member from the bus user groups, two from group transport, four from other user groups and six public interest appointees including, at present, a transport planner, a transport academic, a local councillor, a member of the police service, a lawyer and an accountant. In addition it was decided to establish a trading company to prepare the organisation for the receipt of mainstream services.

Running a commercial London bus route involved a steep learning curve for an organisation whose focus was on community outcomes, rather than financial ones. HCT has grown through identifying needs in the community, testing out small-scale solutions and then growing them into core services. This approach has led to an increase in the range of services being provided by HCT. However, there was also a recognition that long-term sustainability for the organisation could only come from further expansion of service options and a further diversification of funding sources.

Transformation

HCT is a voluntary sector organisation which identifies needs in the local community, tests out small-scale solutions to fulfil them and then grows them into core services. Any initial reservations about the growth of the business, on behalf of commissioners or board members, have been overcome. HCT-run routes consistently outperform routes run by private sector firms.

HCT distinguishes itself from share price-driven bus companies through the provision of family-friendly shifts and encouraging employees to develop new skills. Drivers hold twice-yearly forums with passengers so they can share ideas on how service can be improved.

HCT takes a hard-nosed attitude to the development of surpluses as this is the only way of driving the business forward. The organisation would like to be able to invest in the development of its own asset base. They welcome the introduction of the public interest company which will make it easier for them to raise risk capital and to enable big institutions to invest.

With 20 years' experience working with vulnerable and disabled people, it has the capacity and ability to deliver transport solutions that are in tune with users' needs. That has proved very appealing to local authorities who now come to HCT to help them draw up tenders to ensure that whoever delivers them, the needs of excluded people who will use the transport, are met.

Willow Park

Willow Park is situated in South Manchester, a mile north of Manchester International Airport, near to the city borders with Cheshire. Willow Park Housing Trust is a Large Scale Voluntary Transfer housing association that was set up in 1999 by Manchester City Council, when 90 per cent of tenants in the area voted for it to take over ownership and management of over 6,000 rented homes in East Wythenshawe.

Current nature of provision

Wythenshawe was an area of 30,000 council properties surrounded by affluent areas. Wythenshawe had been designed as a garden suburb but had suffered from poor maintenance and poor management. There was a high level of tenant dissatisfaction with the poor maintenance of properties, a very degraded environment and anti-social behaviour, and public services were run down and underperforming with poor schools, poor health care facilities and poor waste management. Economic restructuring had hit the population hard and those that could, tended to leave the area.

Drivers for change

Manchester Housing was responsible for a very large body of housing across the city. By the mid-1990s, there was an embryonic New Labour administration in the city who wanted to improve the quality of the built environment and lived experience for tenants.

The housing authority in Manchester considered that transfer was the only real option if the housing in the area was going to receive the kind of investment it needed if issues were to be addressed effectively. Champions within the local authority saw the development of a Large Scale Voluntary Transfer (LSVT) association as a well-established model for delivering the necessary investment and providing a platform for improved performance. In addition more localised management would create a closer relationship between the management and residents and provide greater local accountability.

The announcement of the Estates Renewal Challenge Fund (ERCF) for negative-valued housing provided a catalyst for change. Manchester City Housing used the ERCF as an opportunity to lever in capital investment. This allowed for a more strategic approach to be taken to the issue of housing demand and supply, with a modernisation programme to make the area more attractive to new and existing residents.

Attitudes to transfer

A number of stakeholders – the local MP, local councillors, housing authority officers and local groups – came together to work on the options. Tenants were very involved in developing and shaping the 'product'.

The project champions within the local authority knew that they must avoid any accusation of privatisation and the impression of a 'fat-cat' Registered Social Landlord (RSL) being created. So there was a need to manage these anxieties and to keep all stakeholders informed on progress. As a result there was very little opposition to the proposals. However, the process was also less efficient than it might have been because of the complexity of the negotiations.

Trust has been built by allowing tenants to have real influence over the product, by being and staying local, by being responsive and by keeping lines of communication with all stakeholders open and clear.

Business planning

LSVTs have a well-established model for business planning. The initial development group developed a 30-year business plan and sought investment from private sector funders. Given the low value of the properties, the level of anti-social behaviour and the lack of organisational infrastructure, some potential funders, who had invested in previous LSVT proposals, chose not to bid on this occasion.

The level of investment through ERCF was relatively low at £2–3,000 per property. However, the inclusion of pockets of land, community facilities and, crucially, permission to retain receipts from sales has given Willow Park Housing Trust the opportunity to play a wider role and to benefit from the rising land values resulting from the successful regeneration of the area.

The board comprises 15 members with three councillors, one local authority officer, six elected tenants and five independent board members. Whilst there have been changes in the individuals occupying these positions, the stakeholder composition of the board has not particularly changed – although the local authority officer has subsequently been replaced by a local councillor.

The robustness of the business plan has given freedom to innovate and invest in new facilities and projects. Willow Park Housing Trust is able to attract funding that would not be available to the local authority and the new governance structure gives it much more flexibility. It has been lucky in that it undertook a lot of the initial building work during a period of low building inflation. Other LSVTs have not been as fortunate.

Transformation

Since 1999, £70 million has been invested in improvements to homes and the environment, services have been developed and expanded and levels of resident involvement have increased. Population decline has been halted and the area is now attracting a more mixed (and ethnically diverse) community. A key indicator of success has been the reduction in the number of empty homes from 12 per cent in 1999 to 2 per cent in 2004.

There has been a very necessary focus on getting the product right and ensuring that there is a real change in the culture of service delivery to one that is more focused and responsive. New structures for resident involvement have been developed, including a new Area Panel that enables residents to monitor local services and check that rents are being spent on home improvements, local initiatives and new services.

The proximity to Manchester Airport has led to an increase in land values, made the properties more attractive and begun to provide an economic *raison d'être* for the area. The Right to Buy which had been running at a very low level (14 per annum), is now running at 250 a year.

By being in the third sector it has been easier to project an image out into the community and contribute to well-being and community pride. Willow Park Housing Trust has found the inspection regime useful in driving up standards and creating a more customer-focused service. Staff and management have been able to blend the performance-driven culture of the local authority and the customer focus of the voluntary sector to tailor the workload to customer priorities.

Yarrow

Yarrow is a Registered Social Landlord, having achieved registration from the Housing Corporation in November 2001, and is also registered with the Commission for Social Care Inspection. Yarrow seeks to improve the quality of life for individuals with learning disabilities through the provision of individualised care and support solutions including innovative 'day' opportunities and housing solutions so that every service user can live a full, varied and high quality life. In 1992 it took over the running of services for people with learning disabilities, with the resulting transfer of 60 staff from the local NHS Mental Health Trust.

Former nature of provision

The traditional model of care for people with learning difficulties used large-scale institutions, often in the countryside. These provided special accommodation such as registered care homes, usually with shared bedrooms for up to ten people, or long-stay hospitals with wards accommodating 40 people. Those not in such institutions were offered special education for those of school age, or day centre facilities providing occupational therapy for adults.

By the 1980s there was a recognition that this was not meeting the needs and aspirations of people with learning difficulties or their carers. If people with learning difficulties were to lead valued and fulfilled lives, they would need somewhere to live and support to access meaningful daytime occupation and leisure pursuits.

Drivers for change

The needs and aspirations of people with learning difficulties and their families had changed enormously over 30 years. People were living longer and there was an increasing appreciation of what people with learning difficulties could achieve with appropriate support. The NHS was not delivering a particularly medical model in its community homes in Hammersmith and Fulham but it was not responding to the increasing demand for equality, expressed through advocacy and self-advocacy.

By the 1980s there was a huge philosophical push to normalisation. Young staff within the health service wanted to ensure that people with learning disabilities could have the right to an ordinary life and the ability to participate as citizens.

The hospital closure programme provided an impetus. In Hammersmith and Fulham, recognising the underdevelopment in provision for people with learning difficulties, the social services department began to look for smaller-scale provision and had begun to develop employment projects. Increasingly, the case was made that it would be better to provide services at a local level outside the NHS by establishing a new organisation that used different financial models. Above all, commissioners wanted to see the development of more locally based services and cheaper provision.

Attitudes to transfer

Yarrow needed to demonstrate that it was robust enough to manage increased levels of service. The organisation was initially small and informal, housed in the basement of a chiropody clinic, and quickly needed to establish an infrastructure for payroll, office management, office base, HR etc.

Staff were anxious about leaving the 'mothership' of the NHS. The managers and board of Yarrow were concerned that the day of transfer, 1 January 1993, should not be a particularly noteworthy day as far as staff were concerned. There were a number of steps the organisation took to reassure staff by (i) offering an improved working environment, (ii) developing a new common language – it was agreed that as Yarrow called people 'tenants' and the NHS called people 'clients' they would in future be called 'residents', and (iii) ensuring that payroll systems were in place so that there would be a seamless transfer and that the two pay negotiating mechanisms would be merged.

Yarrow decided to register its properties in order to be able to diversify its funding. However, it had no record of running such provision and needed to evidence its ability to do this, and that it was robust enough as an organisation to take on the inherent risks. This also represented a significant level of risk for the NHS and social services. They needed a robust organisation and were willing to provide the investment to allow the organisation to develop. Social services 'placed' local authority councillors on the board as a way of managing this risk.

The board comprised key stakeholders including parents, principal officers from social services and housing, three RSLs, senior managers from within the NHS and two councillors. The board was very aware that the commissioning authorities were taking on significant risks both financially and in terms of the public perception of the new service. Yarrow staff were aware that if they faltered, then the local authority would stop their development.

Business planning

Following the transfer, the board structure changed. Local authority and parent representatives moved on and new board members joined with very different backgrounds and skills. Board members were recruited from the private sector or from people with a strong business orientation. New board members with commercial acumen provide a balance of public sector ethos and private sector motivations.

This has not always been comfortable for those staff who believe that the emphasis of their work should be on caring rather than on managing resources effectively and efficiently. It has also been too entrepreneurial for some board members. The board was initially resistant to extending the geographical area covered by Yarrow – partly because this might lead to a dilution of focus and partly because of capacity issues.

Yarrow is now looking at how users can be more influential in the running of the organisation and are trying to find a way of articulating how this might look. By being located in the voluntary sector Yarrow has been able to be flexible and responsive to the needs of commissioners and users. Yarrow has been able to advise commissioners and lever in resources for the statutory sector and commissioners appear to value Yarrow's expertise and specialist skills.

Transformation

Yarrow has, over the years, extended significantly the range of service models offered to users and commissioners, with an increasing emphasis on people living in their own flats with support. Significant strides have been made towards person-centred planning and particular effort is being made to do this for users with more complex needs in their registered care homes.

Their focus at the beginning was on systematised transition for users. Users are now seeking something different. Yarrow sees its role as helping with social networks in a way that acknowledges the low incomes of most of its residents and the need to maintain their safety. Yarrow would like to move to a model where commissioners pay for the organisation. Service users as 'members' can then, through Direct Payments, pay themselves for the services they want – as you might a gym.

Yarrow's charitable status has enabled it to fundraise and it has been very successful over the years in getting some progressive initiatives funded from charitable donations.

At the outset Yarrow had full cost recovery. However, unless Yarrow is resourced to invest in research and development, there is a sense that this will be eroded and that the continuous transformation that commissioners and users want will be compromised.

Yarrow believes that the real transformation has been in enabling the rights of users and having a business model that is robust enough and flexible enough to respond to their changing needs. Yarrow was allowed the necessary level of investment to be transformative. There is still a push for smaller units of accommodation, but they are more expensive and the organisation is uncertain that it can keep costs low enough to respond effectively.

York Museums Trust

The York Museums Trust (YMT) includes the Castle Museum, the Yorkshire Museum (which had been private until 1961), York St Mary's and the York Art Gallery. In 2002 York City Council transferred the management of the buildings and collections to a charitable trust. The council retains the role of custodian trustee and YMT is the management trustee. YMT is not allowed to sell or dispose of any part of the collection or the estate without first getting the permission of the council. YMT leases the building from the council on a 25-year lease at a peppercorn rent.

Former nature of provision

There were many visitor attractions in York in all sectors. The National Railway Museum is a national collection. The introduction of free entry in 2002 led to a significant increase in visitor numbers. York Minster is arguably a national visitor attraction (with subregional and local stakeholders) and charges visitors for admission. The Minster has experienced some decline in visitors since it introduced charging. The Jorvik Viking Centre, run by the York Archaeological Trust, has a significant profile with the public both in the city and beyond. There are many others.

The Castle Museum, Yorkshire Museum and Art Gallery have good collections but, in spite of generating income from the museums, the local authority had not invested in new material or in the presentation and interpretation of the existing collections. They were still held in affection but had experienced a decline in visitor numbers over a long period.

Drivers for change

There was a perception that all four institutions had become insular and isolated. Whilst there was excellent work being done this was not being promoted effectively. They were not playing a full role in the life of the city or making a full contribution to city-wide partnerships.

The council was concerned that there would be a need for significant investment that they would not be able to resource themselves. A bid to the Heritage Lottery Fund for £10 million was turned down in 1998 and this rejection was a pivotal moment in building the case for change. There was an increasing recognition by councillors of all parties that the council would not find the resources, the drive or the capacity to deliver the necessary programme of change.

A small group of local people with a proven track record in business and enterprise came together to form an 'Initiation Group' with the task of developing the business case for transfer to trust status and to provide the necessary vision to transform the service.

The Initiation Group saw the development of a trust as bringing a number of key advantages:

- It would provide a vehicle for investment and longer-term planning.

- It would locate the management of the service in one place and enable greater efficiency and effectiveness of operation.

- It would enable the recruitment and retention of high calibre staff.

- It would create a service that was visitor focused rather than staff or council focused.

Attitudes to transfer

There was no real opposition to transfer. However, a number of anxieties were expressed:

- from staff about job security and the possibility that institutions might close

- from councillors that public service values would be lost and that the local authority would lose control

- from some academic stakeholders that there would be a 'dumbing down' in the content and presentation of collections.

The proposal to create a charitable trust was critical in building support as all parties recognised that a charitable trust could behave like a public body accountable to stakeholders.

A number of steps were taken to provide reassurance, including the decision that all staff, old and new, could join the North Yorkshire Pension Scheme. This avoided the creation of a two-tier workforce.

Business planning

The first business plan was developed by the Initiation Group. They had no way of knowing the true potential of different parts of the business. The main purpose of this initial business plan was to ensure that there would be long-term investment by the local authority and sufficient levels of funding to provide stability during the period of transfer. They were successful in securing £1.3 million per annum for five years on an annual budget of £3.3 million.

Over time the structure and content of the business plan have changed to take account of:

- balance sheet issues such as cashflow, the need for working capital and a reserves policy

- the need to maximise income from a better use of assets

- the true costs of different operations and activities

- the most effective way of servicing Human Resources, Health and Safety, ICT, Estates and Finance functions.

The board initially comprised representatives of different stakeholder groups with members drawn from the business sector, the local authority (including Lifelong Learning), the museums sector, the arts and the York Philosophical Society. The appointment of local authority councillors as trustees (one from the Labour group and one Liberal Democrat) provided assurance to the authority as custodian trustee that its interests would be protected. Over time, people have been recruited for the contribution that they can bring to the good governance of the organisation. The York Philosophical Society is now the only organisation, other than the local authority, with a 'representative' on the board.

Transformation

YMT has refocused activity to ensure that the constituent parts create a good first impression from local people. This has been achieved through investing in improvements in quality of information and interpretation. There is now one senior management team across the whole organisation. Each site has a manager whose primary responsibility is to deliver a good customer experience. As the organisation brings in new sources of income, staff are being offered packages of resources with which they are encouraged to innovate.

YMT has secured £2 million from voluntary sources in 14 months. Some of this money would have been available to the local authority, but the availability of a dedicated resource means that it has raised more than it might otherwise have done. There are clearly sources of income that would not have come to YMT had it been under local authority control, as well as things like VAT and Gift Aid.

YMT wants to be a major player in the city and now believes that it has a big contribution to make. YMT has already raised the profile of the service and is increasingly visible as a partner in city-wide initiatives. This is already bearing fruit in terms of new partnerships and collaborations.